Merry Christmas
"2007"

From
Dan, Kim & Gideon (to be)
With
All our love!
:)

To

_____

From

_____

Date

_____

365 SPIRIT-LIFTING DEVOTIONS

Hopeful Heart

FIVE-MINUTE DEVOTIONS
FOR WOMEN

Parable
3563 Empleo
St. San Luis Obispo, CA 93401

The quoted ideas expressed in this book (but not Scripture verses) are not, in all cases, exact quotations, as some have been edited for clarity and brevity. In all cases, the author has attempted to maintain the speaker's original intent. In some cases, quoted material for this book was obtained from secondary sources, primarily print media. While every effort was made to ensure the accuracy of these sources, the accuracy cannot be guaranteed. For additions, deletions, corrections, or clarifications in future editions of this text, please write Parable.

The Holy Bible, King James Version

The Holy Bible, New King James Version (NKJV) Copyright © 1982 by Thomas Nelson, Inc. Used by permission.

New Century Version®. (NCV) Copyright © 1987, 1988, 1991 by Word Publishing, a division of Thomas Nelson, Inc. All rights reserved. Used by permission.

The Holman Christian Standard Bible™ (HCSB) Copyright © 1999, 2000, 2001 by Holman Bible Publishers. Used by permission.

The Holy Bible, New International Version®. (NIV) Copyright © 1973, 1978, 1984 International Bible Society. Used by permission of Zondervan. All rights reserved.

The Holy Bible. New Living Translation (NLT) copyright © 1996 Tyndale Charitable Trust. Used by permission of Tyndale House Publishers.

Scripture taken from The Message. (MSG) Copyright © 1993, 1994, 1995, 1996, 2000, 2001, 2002. Used by permission of NavPress Publishing Group.

Cover Design by Kim Russell / Wahoo Designs
Page Layout by Bart Dawson

ISBN-13 978-1-58334-463-7

ISBN-10 1-58334-463-2

Printed in the United States of America

365 SPIRIT-LIFTING DEVOTIONS

Hopeful Heart

FIVE-MINUTE DEVOTIONS
FOR WOMEN

INTRODUCTION

We live in a world where hope is often in short supply. When we focus too intently on the media's avalanche of negative news—or when we become too wrapped up in the inevitable demands and disappointments of everyday life—we can easily fall prey to the pessimism that seems to permeate 21st-century life. But when we focus, instead, on the timeless promises found in God's Holy Word, we are reminded that hope can—and should—belong to all people who are wise enough to entrust their futures to God.

Today and every day, the sun rises upon a world filled with God's presence and His love. As Christians, we have so many reasons to be hopeful: The Father is in His heaven, His love is everlasting, and we, His children, are blessed beyond measure. Yet sometimes we find ourselves distracted by the demands, the frustrations, and the uncertainties of daily life. But even during our darkest days, God never leaves us for an instant. And even when our hopes are dimmed, God's light still shines brightly. As followers of God's Son, we are called to search for that light—and to keep searching for it as long as we live.

This text contains 365 devotional readings that are intended to point you towards God's light by lifting your spirits, lowering your anxieties, raising your hopes, and strengthening your faith. As you read these passages, take time to contemplate your own circumstances, and remember this: Whatever the size of your challenges, God is bigger. Much bigger.

God will instruct you, protect you, energize you, and heal you . . . if you let Him. So be a woman who prays fervently, listens carefully, works diligently, and hopes mightily. Do your best and trust God with the rest. Then, you can rest assured: whatever "it" is, God can handle it . . . and will.

HOPE FOR TODAY,
HOPE FOR TOMORROW

This hope we have as an anchor of the soul, a hope both sure and steadfast.

Hebrews 6:19 NASB

As every woman knows, hope is a perishable commodity. Despite God's promises, despite Christ's love, and despite our countless blessings, we frail human beings can still lose hope from time to time. When we do, we need the encouragement of Christian friends, the life-changing power of prayer, and the healing truth of God's Holy Word.

If we find ourselves falling into the spiritual traps of worry and discouragement, we should seek the healing touch of Jesus and the encouraging words of fellow Christians. Even though this world can be a place of trials and struggles, God has promised us peace, joy, and eternal life if we give ourselves to Him.

Hope looks for the good in people, opens doors for people, discovers what can be done to help, lights a candle, does not yield to cynicism. Hope sets people free.

Barbara Johnson

THE POWER OF FAITH

Have faith in the LORD *your God and you will be upheld.*

2 Chronicles 20:20 NIV

Every life—including yours—is a series of successes and failures, celebrations and disappointments, joys and sorrows. Every step of the way, through every triumph and tragedy, God will stand by your side and strengthen you . . . if you have faith in Him. Jesus taught His disciples that if they had faith, they could move mountains. You can too.

When you place your faith, your trust, indeed your life in the hands of Christ Jesus, you'll be amazed at the marvelous things He can do with you and through you. So strengthen your faith through praise, through worship, through Bible study, and through prayer. And trust God's plans. With Him, all things are possible, and He stands ready to open a world of possibilities to you . . . if you have faith.

Faith never wonders why.

Amy Carmichael

Faith is an act of the will, a choice, based on the unbreakable Word of a God who cannot lie, and who showed what love and obedience and sacrifice mean, in the person of Jesus Christ.

Elisabeth Elliot

THE IMPORTANCE OF PRAYER

Be anxious for nothing, but in everything by prayer and supplication, with thanksgiving, let your requests be made known to God.

Philippians 4:6 NKJV

Prayer is a powerful tool for communicating with our Creator; it is an opportunity to commune with the Giver of all things good. Prayer is not a thing to be taken lightly or to be used infrequently. Prayer should never be reserved for mealtimes or for bedtimes; it should be an ever-present focus in our daily lives.

Daily prayer and meditation is a matter of will and habit. You must willingly organize your time by carving out quiet moments with God, and you must form the habit of daily worship. When you do, you'll discover that no time is more precious than the silent moments you spend with your Heavenly Father.

We must pray literally without ceasing, in every occurrence and employment of our lives. You know I mean that prayer of the heart which is independent of place or situation, or which is, rather, a habit of lifting up the heart to God, as in a constant communication with Him.

Elizabeth Ann Seton

NEW BEGINNINGS

Do not remember the former things, nor consider the things of old. Behold, I will do a new thing.

Isaiah 43:18-19 NKJV

Each new day offers countless opportunities to serve God, to seek His will, and to obey His teachings. But each day also offers countless opportunities to stray from God's commandments and to wander far from His path.

Sometimes, we wander aimlessly in a wilderness of our own making, but God has better plans for us. And, whenever we ask Him to renew our strength and guide our steps, He does so.

Consider this day a new beginning. Consider it a fresh start, a renewed opportunity to serve your Creator with willing hands and a loving heart. Ask God to renew your sense of purpose as He guides your steps. Today is a glorious opportunity to serve your Father in heaven. Seize that opportunity while you can; tomorrow may indeed be too late.

If the leaves had not been let go to fall and wither, if the tree had not consented to be a skeleton for many months, there would be no new life rising, no bud, no flower, no fruit, no seed, no new generation.

Elisabeth Elliot

OPTIMISM NOW!

And now, dear brothers and sisters, let me say one more thing as I close this letter. Fix your thoughts on what is true and honorable and right. Think about things that are pure and lovely and admirable. Think about things that are excellent and worthy of praise.

Philippians 4:8 NLT

As Christian women, we have every reason to rejoice. God is in His heaven; Christ has risen, and we are the sheep of His flock. But, when the demands of life seem great and our resources seem small by comparison, we may find ourselves exhausted, discouraged, or both.

What's your attitude today? Are you fearful, angry, or worried. Are you confused, bitter, or pessimistic? If so, God wants to have a little chat with you.

God wants you to experience His joy and abundance. But, God will not force His joy upon you; you must claim it for yourself. So today, and every day thereafter, celebrate this life that God has given you. Think optimistically about yourself and your future. Give thanks to the One who has given you everything, and trust in your heart that He wants to give you so much more.

Developing a positive attitude means working continually to find what is uplifting and encouraging.

Barbara Johnson

WHAT DOESN'T CHANGE

Jesus Christ is the same yesterday and today and forever.
Hebrews 13:8 NASB

Our world is in a state of constant change. God is not. At times, the world seems to be trembling beneath our feet. But we can be comforted in the knowledge that our Heavenly Father is the rock that cannot be shaken. His Word promises, "I am the Lord, I do not change" (Malachi 3:6 NKJV).

Every day that we live, we mortals encounter a multitude of changes—some good, some not so good, some downright disheartening. On those occasions when us must endure life-changing personal losses that leave us breathless, there is a place we can turn for comfort and assurance—we can turn to God. When we do, our loving Heavenly Father stands ready to protect us, to comfort us, to guide us, and, in time, to heal us.

One of the greatest ways God changes me is by bringing Scripture to mind that I have hidden deep in my heart. And, He always picks the right Scripture at the right time.

Evelyn Christianson

Conditions are always changing; therefore, I must not be dependent upon conditions. What matters supremely is my soul and my relationship to God.

Corrie ten Boom

CLAIMING THE JOY

A cheerful heart has a continual feast.

Proverbs 15:15 HCSB

On some days, as every woman knows, it's hard to be cheerful. Sometimes, as the demands of the world increase and our energy sags, we feel less like "cheering up" and more like "tearing up." But even in our darkest hours, we can turn to God, and He will give us comfort.

Few things in life are more sad, or, for that matter, more absurd, than a grumpy Christian. Christ promises us lives of abundance and joy, but He does not force His joy upon us. We must claim His joy for ourselves, and when we do, Jesus, in turn, fills our spirits with His power and His love.

When we place Jesus at the center of our lives and trust Him as our personal Savior, He will transform us, not just for today, but for all eternity. Then we, as God's children, can share Christ's joy and His message with a world that needs both.

———————

God is good, and heaven is forever. And if those two facts don't cheer you up, nothing will.

Marie T. Freeman

Joy lifts our spirit above earth's sorrow, dancing in jubilation at the hope set before us.

Susan Lenzkes

A LOVE THAT CHANGES EVERYTHING

Your old life is dead. Your new life, which is your real life—even though invisible to spectators—is with Christ in God. He is your life.

What does the love of Christ mean to His believers? It changes everything. His love is perfect and steadfast. Even though we are fallible, and wayward, the Good Shepherd cares for us still. Even though we have fallen far short of the Father's commandments, Christ loves us with a power and depth that is beyond our understanding. And, as we accept Christ's love and walk in Christ's footsteps, our lives bear testimony to His power and to His grace. Yes, Christ's love changes everything; may we invite Him into our hearts so it can then change everything in us.

This hard place in which you perhaps find yourself is the very place in which God is giving you opportunity to look only to Him, to spend time in prayer, and to learn long-suffering, gentleness, meekness—in short, to learn the depths of the love that Christ Himself has poured out on all of us.

Elisabeth Elliot

Our hearts have been made to cry out for a love that can come only from our Creator.

Angela Thomas

NO COMPLAINTS

Do everything without complaining or arguing. Then you will be innocent and without any wrong.

Philippians 2:14-15 NCV

Because we are imperfect human beings, we often lose sight of our blessings. Ironically, most of us have more blessings than we can count, but we may still find reasons to complain about the minor frustrations of everyday life. To do so, of course, is not only wrong; it is also the pinnacle of shortsightedness and a serious roadblock on the path to spiritual abundance.

Are you tempted to complain about the inevitable minor frustrations of everyday living? Don't do it! Today and every day, make it a practice to count your blessings, not your hardships. It's the truly decent way to live.

Thanksgiving or complaining—these words express two contrastive attitudes of the souls of God's children in regard to His dealings with them. The soul that gives thanks can find comfort in everything; the soul that complains can find comfort in nothing.

Hannah Whitall Smith

He wants us to have a faith that does not complain while waiting, but rejoices because we know our times are in His hands—nail-scarred hands that labor for our highest good.

Kay Arthur

A FRESH OPPORTUNITY

When we were baptized, we were buried with Christ and shared his death. So, just as Christ was raised from the dead by the wonderful power of the Father, we also can live a new life.

Romans 6:4 NCV

God's Word is clear: When we genuinely invite Him to reign over our hearts, and when we accept His transforming love, we are forever changed. When we welcome Christ into our hearts, an old life ends and a new way of living—along with a completely new way of viewing the world—begins.

Each morning offers a fresh opportunity to invite Christ, yet once again, to rule over our hearts and our days. Each morning presents yet another opportunity to take up His cross and follow in His footsteps. Today, let us rejoice in the new life that is ours through Christ, and let us follow Him, step by step, on the path that He first walked.

If you are God's child, you are no longer bound to your past or to what you were. You are a brand new creature in Christ Jesus.

Kay Arthur

God specializes in things fresh and firsthand. His plans for you this year may outshine those of the past. He's prepared to fill your days with reasons to give Him praise.

Joni Eareckson Tada

BEYOND THE DAILY GRIND

Are you tired? Worn out? Burned out on religion? Come to me. Get away with me and you'll recover your life. I'll show you how to take a real rest. Walk with me and work with me . . . watch how I do it. Learn the unforced rhythms of grace. I won't lay anything heavy or ill-fitting on you. Keep company with me and you'll learn to live freely and lightly.

Matthew 11:28-30 MSG

Even the most inspired women can, from time to time, find themselves running on empty. Why? Because the inevitable demands of daily life can drain us of our strength and rob us of the joy that is rightfully ours in Christ. Thankfully, God stands ready to renew our spirits, even on the darkest of days. God's Word is clear: When we genuinely lift our hearts and prayers to Him, He renews our strength.

Are you seeking a renewed sense of purpose? Turn your heart toward God in prayer. Are you weak or worried? Take the time to delve deeply into God's Holy Word. Are you spiritually depleted? Call upon fellow believers to support you, and call upon Christ to renew your spirit and your life. When you do, you'll discover that the Creator of the universe stands always ready and always able to create a new sense of wonderment and joy in you.

THE NEED TO BE DISCIPLINED

Do you not know that those who run in a race all run, but only one receives the prize? Run in such a way that you may win. Everyone who competes in the games exercises self-control in all things.

1 Corinthians 9:24-25 NASB

God is clear: we must exercise self-discipline in all matters. Self-discipline is not simply a proven way to get ahead, it's also an integral part of God's plan for our lives. If we genuinely seek to be faithful stewards of our time, our talents, and our resources, we must adopt a disciplined approach to life. Otherwise, our talents are wasted and our resources are squandered.

Our greatest rewards result from hard work and perseverance. May we, as disciplined believers, be willing to work for the rewards we so earnestly desire.

God "longs to be gracious" to us (Isaiah 30:18), and He carries out His judgment against our sin with holy sorrow, intending His discipline to be a vehicle of mercy toward us.

Nancy Groom

If I could just hang in there, being faithful to my own tasks, God would make me joyful and content. The responsibility is mine, but the power is His.

Peg Rankin

CELEBRATING OTHERS

So encourage each other and give each other strength, just as you are doing now.

1 Thessalonians 5:11 NCV

Do you delight in the victories of others? You should. Each day provides countless opportunities to encourage others and to praise their good works. When you do so, you not only spread seeds of joy and happiness, you also obey the commandments of God's Holy Word.

As Christians, we are called upon to spread the Good News of Christ, and we are also called to spread a message of encouragement and hope to the world. So, let us be cheerful Christians with smiles on our faces and encouraging words on our lips. By blessing others, we also bless ourselves, and, at the same time, we do honor to the One who gave His life for us.

My special friends, who know me so well and love me anyway, give me daily encouragement to keep on.

Emilie Barnes

Don't forget that a single sentence, spoken at the right moment, can change somebody's whole perspective on life. A little encouragement can go a long, long way.

Marie T. Freeman

ENTHUSIASTIC SERVICE

Do your work with enthusiasm. Work as if you were serving the Lord, not as if you were serving only men and women.

Ephesians 6:7 NCV

Do you see each day as a glorious opportunity to serve God and to do His will? Are you enthused about life, or do you struggle through each day giving scarcely a thought to God's blessings? Are you constantly praising God for His gifts, and are you sharing His Good News with the world? And are you excited about the possibilities for service that God has placed before you, whether at home, at work, at church, or at school? You should be.

You are the recipient of Christ's sacrificial love. Accept it enthusiastically and share it fervently. Jesus deserves your enthusiasm; the world deserves it; and you deserve the experience of sharing it.

The proper perspective creates within us a spirit of reaching outside of ourselves with joy and enthusiasm.

Luci Swindoll

God wants us to serve Him with a willing spirit, one that would choose no other way.

Beth Moore

THE MASTER'S TOUCH

Everything is possible to the one who believes.

Mark 9:23 HCSB

When a suffering woman sought healing by simply touching the hem of His garment, Jesus turned and said, "Daughter, be of good comfort; thy faith hath made thee whole" (Matthew 9:22 KJV). We, too, can be made whole when we place our faith completely and unwaveringly in the person of Jesus Christ.

Concentration camp survivor Corrie ten Boom relied on faith during her ten months of imprisonment and torture. Later, despite the fact that four of her family members had died in Nazi death camps, Corrie's faith was unshaken. She wrote, "There is no pit so deep that God's love is not deeper still." Christians take note: Genuine faith in God means faith in all circumstances, happy or sad, joyful or tragic.

If your faith is being tested to the point of breaking, know that your Savior is near. If you reach out to Him in faith, He will give you peace and heal your broken spirit. Be content to touch even the smallest fragment of the Master's garment, and He will make you whole.

Faith is our spiritual oxygen. It not only keeps us alive in God, but enables us to grow stronger . . . .

Joyce Landorf Heatherly

BUILDING FELLOWSHIP

It is good and pleasant when God's people live together in peace!

Psalm 133:1 NCV

Fellowship with other believers should be an integral part of your everyday life. Your association with fellow Christians should be uplifting, enlightening, encouraging, and consistent.

Are you an active member of your own fellowship? Are you a builder of bridges inside the four walls of your church and outside it? Do you contribute to God's glory by contributing your time and your talents to a close-knit band of believers? Hopefully so. The fellowship of believers is intended to be a powerful tool for spreading God's Good News and uplifting His children. And God intends for you to be a fully contributing member of that fellowship. Your intentions should be the same.

Be united with other Christians. A wall with loose bricks is not good. The bricks must be cemented together.

Corrie ten Boom

One of the ways God refills us after failure is through the blessing of Christian fellowship. Just experiencing the joy of simple activities shared with other children of God can have a healing effect on us.

Anne Graham Lotz

EXTREME CHANGES

Then He said to them all, "If anyone wants to come with Me, he must deny himself, take up his cross daily, and follow Me."

Luke 9:23 HCSB

Jesus made an extreme sacrifice for you. Are you willing to make extreme changes in your life for Him? Can you honestly say that you're passionate about your faith and that you're really following Jesus? Hopefully so. But if you're preoccupied with other things—or if you're strictly a one-day-a-week Christian—then you're in need of an extreme spiritual makeover!

Nothing is more important than your whole-hearted commitment to your Creator and to His only begotten Son. Your faith must never be an afterthought; it must be your ultimate priority, your ultimate possession, and your ultimate passion. You are the recipient of Christ's love. Accept it enthusiastically and share it passionately. Jesus deserves your extreme enthusiasm; the world deserves it; and you deserve the experience of sharing it.

————————

The Christian faith is meant to be lived moment by moment. It isn't some broad, general outline—it's a long walk with a real Person. Details count: passing thoughts, small sacrifices, a few encouraging words, little acts of kindness, brief victories over nagging sins.

Joni Eareckson Tada

FRIENDSHIPS
THAT HONOR GOD

If your life honors the name of Jesus, he will honor you.
2 Thessalonians 1:12 MSG

Some friendships help us honor God; these friendships should be nurtured. Other friendships place us in situations where we are tempted to dishonor God by disobeying His commandments; friendships such as these have the potential to do us great harm.

Because we tend to become like our friends, we must choose our friends carefully. Because our friends influence us in ways that are both subtle and powerful, we must ensure that our friendships are pleasing to God. When we spend our days in the presence of godly believers, we are blessed, not only by those friends, but also by our Creator.

———————

Friends are like a quilt with lots of different shapes, sizes, colors, and patterns of fabric. But the end result brings you warmth and comfort in a support system that makes your life richer and fuller.

Suzanne Dale Ezell

Insomuch as any one pushes you nearer to God, he or she is your friend.

Anonymous

THE MIRACLE WORKER

Jesus said to them, "I have shown you many great miracles from the Father."

John 10:32 NIV

God is a miracle worker. Throughout history He has intervened in the course of human events in ways that cannot be explained by science or human rationale. And He's still doing so today.

God's miracles are not limited to special occasions, nor are they witnessed by a select few. God is crafting His wonders all around us: the miracle of the birth of a new baby; the miracle of a world renewing itself with every sunrise; the miracle of lives transformed by God's love and grace. Each day, God's handiwork is evident for all to see and experience.

Today, seize the opportunity to inspect God's hand at work. His miracles come in a variety of shapes and sizes, so keep your eyes and your heart open. Be watchful, and you'll soon be amazed.

I believe that God is in the miracle business—that his favorite way of working is to pick up where our human abilities and understandings leave off and then do something so wondrous and unexpected that there's no doubt who the God is around here.

Emilie Barnes

THIS IS HIS DAY

This is the day the LORD has made. We will rejoice and be glad in it.

Psalm 118:24 NLT

The 118th Psalm reminds us that today, like every other day, is a cause for celebration. God gives us this day; He fills it to the brim with possibilities, and He challenges us to use it for His purposes. The day is presented to us fresh and clean at midnight, free of charge, but we must beware: Today is a non-renewable resource—once it's gone, it's gone forever. Our responsibility, of course, is to use this day in the service of God's will and according to His commandments.

Today, treasure the time that God has given you. Give Him the glory and the praise and the thanksgiving that He deserves. And search for the hidden possibilities that God has placed along your path. This day is a priceless gift from God, so use it joyfully and encourage others to do likewise. After all, this is the day the Lord has made . . . .

Not every day of our lives is overflowing with joy and celebration. But there are moments when our hearts nearly burst within us for the sheer joy of being alive. The first sight of our newborn babies, the warmth of love in another's eyes, the fresh scent of rain on a hot summer's eve—moments like these renew in us a heartfelt appreciation for life.

Gwen Ellis

CHARACTER-BUILDING TAKES TIME

Applying all diligence, in your faith supply moral excellence.

2 Peter 1:5 NASB

Character is built slowly over a lifetime. It is the sum of every right decision, every honest word, every noble thought, and every heartfelt prayer. It is forged on the anvil of honorable work and polished by the twin virtues of generosity and humility. Character is a precious thing—difficult to build but easy to tear down.

As believers in Christ, we must seek to live each day with discipline, honesty, and faith. When we do, integrity becomes a habit. And God smiles.

There is something about having endured great loss that brings purity of purpose and strength of character.

Barbara Johnson

Often, our character is at greater risk in prosperity than in adversity.

Beth Moore

A PRAYER

Heavenly Father, Your Word instructs me to walk in righteousness and in truth. Make me Your worthy servant, Lord. Let my words be true, and let my actions lead others to You. Amen

CHOICES THAT PLEASE GOD

I am offering you life or death, blessings or curses. Now, choose life! . . . To choose life is to love the Lord your God, obey him, and stay close to him.

Deuteronomy 30:19-20 NCV

Sometimes, because you're an imperfect human being, you may become so wrapped up in meeting society's expectations that you fail to focus on God's expectations. To do so is a mistake of major proportions—don't make it. Instead, seek God's guidance as you focus your energies on becoming the best "you" that you can possibly be. And, when it comes to matters of conscience, seek approval not from your peers, but from your Creator.

Whom will you try to please today: God or man? Your primary obligation is not to please imperfect men and women. Your obligation is to strive diligently to meet the expectations of an all-knowing and perfect God. Trust Him always. Love Him always. Praise Him always. And make choices that please Him. Always.

The location of your affections will drive the direction of your decisions.

Lisa Bevere

Freedom is not the right to do what we want but the power to do what we ought.

Corrie ten Boom

MEASURING YOUR WORDS

From a wise mind comes wise speech; the words of the wise are persuasive.

Proverbs 16:23 NLT

God's Word reminds us that "Reckless words pierce like a sword, but the tongue of the wise brings healing" (Proverbs 12:18 NIV). If you seek to be a source of encouragement to friends, to family members and to coworkers, then you must measure your words carefully. And that's exactly what God wants you to do.

Today, make this promise to yourself: vow to be an honest, effective, encouraging communicator at work, at home, and everyplace in between. Speak wisely, not impulsively. Use words of kindness and praise, not words of anger or derision. Learn how to be truthful without being cruel. Remember that you have the power to heal others or to injure them, to lift others up or to hold them back. And when you learn how to lift them up, you'll soon discover that you've lifted yourself up, too.

———————

Keeping the lines of communication open can help exterminate the pests that gnaw away at love.

Annie Chapman

GOD'S ASSURANCE

I've told you all this so that trusting me, you will be unshakable and assured, deeply at peace. In this godless world you will continue to experience difficulties. But take heart! I've conquered the world.

John 16:33 MSG

Are you a confident believer, or do you live under a cloud of uncertainty and doubt? As a Christian, you have many reasons to be confident. After all, God is in His heaven; Christ has risen; and you are the recipient of God's grace. Despite these blessings, you may, from time to time, find yourself being tormented by negative emotions—and you are certainly not alone.

Even the most faithful Christians are overcome by occasional bouts of fear and doubt. You are no different.

But even when you feel very distant from God, remember that God is never distant from you. When you sincerely seek His presence, He will touch your heart, calm your fears, and restore your confidence.

Yes, we need to acknowledge our weaknesses, to confess our sins. But if we want to be active, productive participants in the realm of God, we also need to recognize our gifts, to appreciate our strengths, to build on the abilities God has given us. We need to balance humility with confidence.

Penelope Stokes

THE STORMS OF LIFE

But Jesus immediately said to them: "Take courage! It is I. Don't be afraid."

Matthew 14:27 NIV

A storm rose quickly on the Sea of Galilee, and the disciples were afraid. Although they had seen Jesus perform many miracles, the disciples feared for their lives, so they turned to their Savior, and He calmed the waters and the wind.

Sometimes, we, like the disciples, feel threatened by the inevitable storms of life. And when we are fearful, we, too, can turn to Christ for courage and for comfort.

The next time you're afraid, remember that the One who calmed the wind and the waves is also your personal Savior. And remember that the ultimate battle has already been won at Calvary. We, as believers, can live courageously in the promises of our Lord . . . and we should.

Recently I've been learning that life comes down to this: God is in everything. Regardless of what difficulties I am experiencing at the moment, or what things aren't as I would like them to be, I look at the circumstances and say, "Lord, what are you trying to teach me?"

Catherine Marshall

LETTING GOD DECIDE

A man's heart plans his way, but the Lord directs his steps.

Proverbs 16:9 NKJV

Are you facing a difficult decision, a troubling circumstance, or a powerful temptation? If so, it's time to step back, to stop focusing on the world, and to focus, instead, on the will of your Father in heaven. The world will often lead you astray, but God will not. His counsel leads you to Himself, which, of course, is the path He has always intended for you to take.

Everyday living is an exercise in decision-making. Today and every day you must make choices: choices about what you will do, what you will worship, and how you will think. When in doubt, make choices that you sincerely believe will bring you to a closer relationship with God. And if you're uncertain of your next step, pray about it. When you do, answers will come—the right answers for you.

No trumpets sound when the important decisions of our life are made. Destiny is made known silently.

Agnes DeMille

A PRAYER

Lord, help me to make decisions that are pleasing to You. Help me to be honest, patient, thoughtful, and obedient. And above all, help me to follow the teachings of Jesus, not just today, but every day. Amen

DISCIPLINE YOURSELF

Discipline yourself for the purpose of godliness.

1 Timothy 4:7 NASB

Are you a self-disciplined woman? If so, congratulations . . . your disciplined approach to life can help you build a more meaningful relationship with God. Why? Because God expects all His believers (including you) to lead lives of disciplined obedience to Him . . . and He rewards those believers who do.

Sometimes, it's hard to be dignified and disciplined. Why? Because you live in a world where many prominent people want you to believe that dignified, self-disciplined behavior is going out of style. But don't deceive yourself: self-discipline never goes out of style.

Your greatest accomplishments will probably require heaping helpings of self-discipline—which, by the way, is perfectly fine with God. After all, He knows that you're up to the task, and He has big plans for you. God will do His part to fulfill those plans, and the rest, of course, depends upon you.

Real freedom means to welcome the responsibility it brings, to welcome the God-control it requires, to welcome the discipline that results, to welcome the maturity it creates.

Eugenia Price

PATS ON THE BACK

So let us try to do what makes peace and helps one another.

Romans 14:19 NCV

Life is a team sport, and all of us need occasional pats on the back from our teammates. In the book of Ephesians, Paul writes, "Do not let any unwholesome talk come out of your mouths, but only what is helpful for building others up according to their needs, that it may benefit those who listen" (4:29 NIV). Paul reminds us that when we choose our words carefully, we can have a powerful impact on those around us.

Since we don't always know who needs our help, the best strategy is to encourage all the people who cross our paths. So today, be a world-class source of encouragement to everyone you meet. Never has the need been greater.

Encouragement is to a friendship what confetti is to a party.

Nicole Johnson

Once you loosen up, let yourself be who you are: the wonderful, witty woman whom God will use to encourage and uplift other people.

Barbara Johnson

GOD'S ALLY

Be self-controlled and alert. Your enemy the devil prowls around like a roaring lion looking for someone to devour. Resist him, standing firm in the faith . . . .

1 Peter 5:8-9 NIV

Nineteenth-century clergyman Edwin Hubbel Chapin warned, "Neutral people are the devil's allies." His words were true then, and they're true now. Neutrality in the face of evil is a sin. Yet all too often, we fail to fight evil, not because we are neutral, but because we are shortsighted: we don't fight the devil because we don't recognize his handiwork.

If we are to recognize evil and fight it, we must pay careful attention. We must pay attention to God's Word, and we must pay attention to the realities of everyday life. When we observe life objectively, and when we do so with eyes and hearts that are attuned to God's Holy Word, we can no longer be neutral believers. And when we are no longer neutral, God rejoices while the devil despairs.

We are in a continual battle with the spiritual forces of evil, but we will triumph when we yield to God's leading and call on His powerful presence in prayer.

Shirley Dobson

IN HIS HANDS

For whatever is born of God overcomes the world. And this is the victory that has overcome the world—our faith.

1 John 5:4 NKJV

The first element of a successful life is faith: faith in God, faith in His Son, and faith in His promises. If we place our lives in God's hands, our faith is rewarded in ways that we—as human beings with clouded vision and limited understanding—can scarcely comprehend. But, if we seek to rely solely upon our own resources, or if we seek earthly success outside the boundaries of God's commandments, we reap a bitter harvest for ourselves and for our loved ones.

Do you desire the abundance and success that God has promised? Then trust Him today and every day that you live. Then, when you have entrusted your future to the Giver of all things good, rest assured that your future is secure, not only for today, but also for all eternity.

O holy Savior, Friend unseen, the faint, the weak on Thee may lean, help me, throughout life's varying scene, by faith to cling to Thee.

Charlotte Elliott

THE LAST WORD

For God has not given us a spirit of fear and timidity, but of power, love, and self-discipline. So you must never be ashamed to tell others about our Lord.

2 Timothy 1:7-8 NLT

All of us may find our courage tested by the inevitable disappointments and tragedies of life. After all, ours is a world filled with uncertainty, hardship, sickness, and danger. Old Man Trouble, it seems, is never too far from the front door.

When we focus upon our fears and our doubts, we may find many reasons to lie awake at night and fret about the uncertainties of the coming day. A better strategy, of course, is to focus not upon our fears, but instead upon our God.

God is your shield and your strength; you are His forever. So don't focus your thoughts upon the fears of the day. Instead, trust God's plan and His eternal love for you. And remember: God is good, and He has the last word.

I have found the perfect antidote for fear. Whenever it sticks up its ugly face, I clobber it with prayer.

Dale Evans Rogers

A PRAYER

Thank You, Lord, for Your perfect love, a love that casts out fear and gives me strength and courage to meet the challenges of this world. Amen

IN THE FOOTSTEPS
OF THE SAVIOR

Whoever serves me must follow me. Then my servant will be with me everywhere I am. My Father will honor anyone who serves me.

John 12:26 NCV

Whom will you walk with today? Will you walk with people who worship the ways of the world? Or will you walk with the Son of God? Jesus walks with you. Are you walking with Him? Hopefully, you will choose to walk with Him today and every day of your life. God's Word promises that when you follow in Christ's footsteps, you will learn how to live freely and lightly (Matthew 11:28-30).

Are you worried about the day ahead? Be confident in God's power. He will never desert you. Are you concerned about the future? Be courageous and call upon God. He will protect you. Are you confused? Listen to the quiet voice of your Heavenly Father. He is not a God of confusion. So talk with God; listen to Him; and walk with His Son—starting now.

We are meddling with God's business when we let all manner of imaginings loose, predicting disaster, contemplating possibilities instead of following, one day at a time, God's plain and simple pathway.

Elisabeth Elliot

PERFECT WISDOM

Therefore everyone who hears these words of mine and puts them into practice is like a wise man who built his house on the rock.

Matthew 7:24-25 NIV

Where will you place your trust today? Will you trust in the wisdom of fallible men and women, or will you place your faith in God's perfect wisdom? Where you choose to place your trust will determine the direction and quality of your life.

Are you tired? Discouraged? Fearful? Be comforted and trust God. Are you worried or anxious? Be confident in God's power and trust His Holy Word. Are you confused? Listen to the quiet voice of your Heavenly Father. He is not a God of confusion. Talk with Him; listen to Him; trust Him. He is steadfast, and He is your protector . . . forever.

———————

Decisions which are made in the light of God's Word are stable and show wisdom.

Vonette Bright

Wisdom always waits for the right time to act, while emotion always pushes for action right now.

Joyce Meyer

USING YOUR GIFTS

I remind you to fan into flame the gift of God.
2 Timothy 1:6 NIV

All women possess special gifts and talents; you are no exception. But, your gift is no guarantee of success; it must be cultivated and nurtured; otherwise, it will go unused . . . and God's gift to you will be squandered.

Today, accept this challenge: value the talent that God has given you, nourish it, make it grow, and share it with the world. After all, the best way to say "Thank You" for God's gift is to use it.

It is the definition of joy to be able to offer back to God the essence of what he's placed in you, be that creativity or a love of ideas or a compassionate heart or the gift of hospitality.

Paula Rinehart

What we are is God's gift to us. What we become is our gift to God.

Anonymous

A PRAYER

Heavenly Father, Your gifts to me are priceless and eternal. I praise You and give thanks for Your creation, for Your Son, and for the unique talents and opportunities that You have given me. Let me use my gifts for the glory of Your kingdom, today and every day. Amen

WHY HE SENT HIS SON

*For all have sinned and fall short of the glory of God,
and are justified freely by his grace through the redemption
that came by Christ Jesus.*

Romans 3:23-24 NIV

Despite our shortcomings, God sent His Son so that we might be redeemed from our sins. In doing so, our Heavenly Father demonstrated His infinite mercy and His infinite love. We have received countless gifts from God, but none can compare with the gift of salvation. God's grace is the ultimate gift, and we owe Him the ultimate in thanksgiving.

Christ sacrificed His life on the cross so that we might have eternal life. This gift, freely given from God's only begotten Son, is the priceless possession of everyone who accepts Him as Lord and Savior. We return our Savior's love by welcoming Him into our hearts and sharing His message and His love. When we do so, we are blessed here on earth and throughout all eternity.

God "longs to be gracious" to us (Isaiah 30:18), and He carries out His judgment against our sin with holy sorrow, intending His discipline to be a vehicle of mercy toward us.

Nancy Groom

OUR FAITH, HIS PROMISES

Let's keep a firm grip on the promises that keep us going.
He always keeps his word.

Hebrews 10:23 MSG

The Christian faith is founded upon promises that are contained in a unique book. That book is the Holy Bible. The Bible is a roadmap for life here on earth and for life eternal. As Christians, we are called upon to study its meaning, to trust its promises, to follow its commandments, and to share its Good News. God's Holy Word is, indeed, a transforming, one-of-a-kind treasure, and must be treated that way.

God has made promises to you, and He intends to keep them. So take God at His word: trust His promises and share them with your family, with your friends, and with the world.

———————

Shake the dust from your past, and move forward in His promises.

Kay Arthur

Claim all of God's promises in the Bible. Your sins, your worries, your life—you may cast them all on Him.

Corrie ten Boom

TRUSTING HIS TIMING

He told them, "You don't get to know the time. Timing is the Father's business."

Acts 1:7 MSG

If you sincerely seek to be a woman of faith, then you must learn to trust God's timing. You will be sorely tempted, however, to do otherwise. Because you are a fallible human being, you are impatient for things to happen. But, God knows better.

God has created a world that unfolds according to His own timetable, not ours . . . thank goodness! We mortals might make a terrible mess of things. God does not.

God's plan does not always happen in the way that we would like or at the time of our own choosing. Our task—as believing Christians who trust in a benevolent, all-knowing Father—is to wait patiently for God to reveal Himself. And reveal Himself He will. Always. But until God's perfect plan is made known, we must walk in faith and never lose hope. And we must continue to trust Him. Always.

We must leave it to God to answer our prayers in His own wisest way. Sometimes, we are so impatient and think that God does not answer. God always answers! He never fails! Be still. Abide in Him.

Mrs. Charles E. Cowman

HOW BEST TO TREAT OTHERS

Here is a simple, rule-of-thumb for behavior: Ask yourself what you want people to do for you, then grab the initiative and do it for them. Add up God's Law and Prophets and this is what you get.

Matthew 7:12 MSG

Would you like to make the world a better place? If so, you can start by practicing the Golden Rule.

Is the Golden Rule your rule, or is it just another Bible verse that goes in one ear and out the other? Jesus made Himself perfectly clear: He instructed you to treat other people in the same way that you want to be treated. But sometimes, especially when you're feeling the pressures of everyday living, obeying the Golden Rule can seem like an impossible task—but it's not. So if you want to know how to treat other people, ask the person you see every time you look into the mirror. The answer you receive will tell you exactly what to do.

It is one of the most beautiful compensations of life that no one can sincerely try to help another without helping herself.

Barbara Johnson

HIS JOY . . . AND OURS

Always be full of joy in the Lord. I say it again—rejoice!
Philippians 4:4 NLT

Christ made it clear: He intends that His joy should become our joy. Yet sometimes, amid the inevitable hustle and bustle of life-here-on-earth, we can forfeit—albeit temporarily—the joy of Christ as we wrestle with the challenges of daily living.

Corrie ten Boom correctly observed, "Jesus did not promise to change the circumstances around us. He promised great peace and pure joy to those who would learn to believe that God actually controls all things." So here's a prescription for better spiritual health: Learn to trust God, and open the door of your soul to Christ. When you do, He will most certainly give you the peace and pure joy He has promised.

———————

It is the definition of joy to be able to offer back to God the essence of what he's placed in you, be that creativity or a love of ideas or a compassionate heart or the gift of hospitality.

Paula Rinehart

A PRAYER

Dear Lord, You have created a glorious universe that is far beyond my understanding. You have given me the gift of Your Son and the gift of salvation. Let me be a joyful Christian, Lord, this day and every day. Today is Your gift to me. Let me use it to Your glory as I give all the praise to You. Amen

CHOOSING KINDNESS

A kind man benefits himself, but a cruel man brings disaster on himself.

Proverbs 11:17 HCSB

If we believe the words of Proverbs 11:17—and we should—then we understand that kindness is its own reward. And, if we obey the commandments of our Savior—and we should—we must sow seeds of kindness wherever we go.

Kindness is a choice. Sometimes, when we feel happy or generous, we find it easy to be kind. Other times, when we are discouraged or tired, we can scarcely summon the energy to utter a single kind word. But, God's commandment is clear: He intends that we make the conscious choice to treat others with kindness and respect, no matter our circumstances, no matter our emotions. Kindness, therefore, is a choice that we, as Christians must make many times each day.

As much as God loves to hear our worship and adoration, surely he delights all the more in seeing our gratitude translated into simple kindnesses that keep the chain of praise unbroken, alive in others' hearts.

Evelyn Christenson

YOUR SHINING LIGHT

While ye have light, believe in the light, that ye may be the children of light.

John 12:36 KJV

The Bible says that you are "the light that gives light to the world." What kind of light have you been giving off? Hopefully, you've been a good example for everybody to see. Why? Because the world needs all the light it can get, and that includes your light, too!

Christ showed enduring love for you by willingly sacrificing His own life so that you might have eternal life. As a response to His sacrifice, you should love Him, praise Him, and share His message of salvation with your neighbors and with the world. So let your light shine today and every day. When you do, God will bless you now and forever.

Light is stronger than darkness—darkness cannot "comprehend" or "overcome" it.

Anne Graham Lotz

His life is our light—our purpose and meaning and reason for living.

Anne Graham Lotz

NEW BEGINNINGS

I will give you a new heart and put a new spirit in you . . . .

Ezekiel 36:26 NIV

If we sincerely want to change ourselves for the better, we must start on the inside and work our way out from there. Lasting change doesn't occur "out there"; it occurs "in here." It occurs, not in the shifting sands of our own particular circumstances, but in the quiet depths of our own hearts.

Are you in search of a new beginning or, for that matter, a new you? If so, don't expect changing circumstances to miraculously transform you into the person you want to become. Transformation starts with God, and it starts in the silent center of a humble human heart—like yours.

In those desperate times when we feel like we don't have an ounce of strength, He will gently pick up our heads so that our eyes can behold something— something that will keep His hope alive in us.

Kathy Troccoli

There is so much Heaven around us now if we have eyes for it, because eternity starts when we give ourselves to God.

Gloria Gaither

CALMNESS IN CHAOS

Thou wilt keep him in perfect peace, whose mind is stayed on thee.

Isaiah 26:3 KJV

The beautiful words of John 14:27 give us hope: "Peace I leave with you, my peace I give unto you . . . ." Jesus offers us peace, not as the world gives, but as He alone gives. We, as believers, can accept His peace or ignore it.

When we accept the peace of Jesus Christ into our hearts, our lives are transformed. And then, because we possess the gift of peace, we can share that gift with fellow Christians, family members, friends, and associates. If, on the other hand, we choose to ignore the gift of peace—for whatever reason—we cannot share what we do not possess.

As every woman knows, peace can be a scarce commodity in a demanding, 21st-century world. How, then, can we find the peace that we so desperately desire? By turning our days and our lives over to God. Elisabeth Elliot writes, "If my life is surrendered to God, all is well. Let me not grab it back, as though it were in peril in His hand but would be safer in mine!" May we give our lives, our hopes, and our prayers to the Lord, and, by doing so, accept His will and His peace.

PRAISE HIM

Praise the LORD. *Give thanks to the* LORD, *for he is good;
his love endures forever.*

Psalm 106:1 NIV

Sometimes, in our rush "to get things done," we simply don't stop long enough to pause and thank our Creator for the countless blessings He has bestowed upon us. But when we slow down and express our gratitude to the One who made us, we enrich our own lives and the lives of those around us.

Thanksgiving should become a habit, a regular part of our daily routines. God has blessed us beyond measure, and we owe Him everything, including our eternal praise. Let us praise Him today, tomorrow, and throughout eternity.

Praise Him! Praise Him! Tell of His excellent greatness. Praise Him! Praise Him! Ever in joyful song!

Fanny Crosby

The time for universal praise is sure to come some day. Let us begin to do our part now.

Hannah Whitall Smith

A PRAYER

Heavenly Father, today and every day I will praise You. I will praise You with my thoughts, my prayers, my words, and my deeds . . . now and forever. Amen

TAKING RISKS

Is anything too hard for the Lord?

Genesis 18:14 NKJV

As we consider the uncertainties of the future, we are confronted with a powerful temptation: the temptation to "play it safe." Unwilling to move mountains, we fret over molehills. Unwilling to entertain great hopes for tomorrow, we focus on the unfairness of today. Unwilling to trust God completely, we take timid half-steps when God intends that we make giant leaps.

Today, ask God for the courage to step beyond the boundaries of your doubts. Ask Him to guide you to a place where you can realize your full potential—a place where you are freed from the fear of failure. Ask Him to do His part, and promise Him that you will do your part. Don't ask Him to lead you to a "safe" place; ask Him to lead you to the "right" place . . . and remember: those two places are seldom the same.

God is teaching me to become more and more "teachable": To keep evolving. To keep taking the risk of learning something new . . . or unlearning something old and off base.

Beth Moore

A PRESCRIPTION FOR PANIC

Anxiety in the heart of man causes depression, but a good word makes it glad.

Proverbs 12:25 NKJV

We are members of an anxious society, a society in which the changes we face threaten to outpace our abilities to make adjustments. No wonder we sometimes find ourselves beset by feelings of anxiety and panic.

At times, our anxieties may stem from physical causes—chemical imbalances in the brain that result in severe emotional distress or relentless panic attacks. In such cases, modern medicine offers hope to those who suffer. But oftentimes, our anxieties result from spiritual deficits, not physical ones. And when we're spiritually depleted, the best prescription is found not in the medicine cabinet but deep inside the human heart. What we need is a higher daily dose of God's love, God's peace, God's assurance, and God's presence. And how do we acquire these blessings from our Creator? Through prayer, through meditation, through worship, and through trust.

He treats us as sons, and all he asks in return is that we shall treat Him as a Father whom we can trust without anxiety. We must take the son's place of dependence and trust, and we must let Him keep the father's place of care and responsibility.

Hannah Whitall Smith

FACING UP TO TROUBLE

When you go through deep waters and great trouble, I will be with you. When you go through the rivers of difficulty, you will not drown! When you walk through the fire of oppression, you will not be burned up; the flames will not consume you. For I am the Lord, your God . . . .

Isaiah 43:2-3 NLT

As life-here-on-earth unfolds, all of us encounter occasional setbacks: Those occasional visits from Old Man Trouble are simply a fact of life, and none of us are exempt. When tough times arrive, we may be forced to rearrange our plans and our priorities. But even on our darkest days, we must remember that God's love remains constant.

The fact that we encounter adversity is not nearly so important as the way we choose to deal with it. When tough times arrive, we have a clear choice: we can begin the difficult work of tackling our troubles . . . or not. When we summon the courage to look Old Man Trouble squarely in the eye, an amazing thing usually happens: he blinks.

We all go through pain and sorrow, but the presence of God, like a warm, comforting blanket, can shield us and protect us, and allow the deep inner joy to surface, even in the most devastating circumstances.

Barbara Johnson

OUR ROCK

*And he said: "The Lord is my rock and my fortress and
my deliverer; the God of my strength, in whom I will
trust."*

2 Samuel 22:2-3 NKJV

Psalm 145 promises, "The Lord is near to all who
call on him, to all who call on him in truth. He fulfills
the desires of those who fear him; he hears their cry
and saves them" (vv. 18-20 NIV). And the words of
Jesus offer us comfort: "These things I have spoken
to you, that in Me you may have peace. In the world
you will have tribulation; but be of good cheer, I have
overcome the world" (John 16:33 NKJV).

As believers, we know that God loves us and
that He will protect us. In times of hardship, He will
comfort us; in times of sorrow, He will dry our tears.
When we are troubled or weak or sorrowful, God is
always with us. We must build our lives on the rock
that cannot be shaken: we must trust in God. And
then, we must get on with the hard work of tackling
our problems . . . because if we don't, who will? Or
should?

When I feel like circumstances are spiraling
downward in my life, God taught me that whether
I'm right side up or upside down, I need to turn those
circumstances over to Him. He is the only one who
can bring balance into my life.

Carole Lewis

WHEN MOUNTAINS MOVE

You do not have, because you do not ask God.

James 4:2 NIV

God gives the gifts; we, as believers, should accept them—but oftentimes, we don't. Why? Because we fail to trust our Heavenly Father completely, and because we are, at times, surprisingly stubborn. Luke 11 teaches us that God does not withhold spiritual gifts from those who ask. Our obligation, quite simply, is to ask for them.

Are you a woman who asks God to move mountains in your life, or are you expecting Him to stumble over molehills? Whatever the size of your challenges, God is big enough to handle them. Ask for His help today, with faith and with fervor, and then watch in amazement as your mountains begin to move.

God uses our most stumbling, faltering faith-steps as the open door to His doing for us "more than we ask or think."

Catherine Marshall

Jesus taught that the evidence that confirms our leaps of faith comes after we risk believing, not before.

Gloria Gaither

BELIEVING MAKES
A DIFFERENCE

You love Him, though you have not seen Him. And though not seeing Him now, you believe in Him and rejoice with inexpressible and glorious joy, because you are receiving the goal of your faith, the salvation of your souls.

1 Peter 1:8-9 HCSB

If you'd like to partake in the peace that only God can give, make certain that your actions are guided by His Word. And while you're at it, pay careful attention to the conscience that God, in His infinite wisdom, has placed in your heart. Don't treat your faith as if it were separate from your everyday life. Weave your beliefs into the very fabric of your day. When you do, God will honor your good works, and your good works will honor God.

If you seek to be a responsible believer, you must realize that it is never enough to hear the instructions of God; you must also live by them. And it is never enough to wait idly by while others do God's work here on earth; you, too, must act. Doing God's work is a responsibility that every Christian (including you) should bear. And when you do, your loving Heavenly Father will reward your efforts with a bountiful harvest.

If all things are possible with God, then all things are possible to him who believes in him.

Corrie ten Boom

BLESSED BEYOND MEASURE

The Lord bless you and keep you; The Lord make His face shine upon you, And be gracious to you.

Numbers 6:24-25 NKJV

Have you counted your blessings lately? You should. Of course, God's gifts are too numerous to count, but as a grateful Christian, you should attempt to count them nonetheless. Your blessings include life, family, friends, talents, and possessions, for starters. And your greatest gift—a treasure that was paid for on the cross and is yours for the asking—is God's gift of salvation through Christ Jesus.

As believing Christians, we have all been blessed beyond measure. Thus, thanksgiving should become a habit, a regular part of our daily routines. Today, let us pause and thank our Creator for His blessings. And let us demonstrate our gratitude to the Giver of all things good by using His gifts for the glory of His kingdom.

God is always far more willing to give us good things than we are anxious to have them.

Catherine Marshall

The Bible plainly teaches that if we will learn and act on the Word, God will bless our lives.

Joyce Meyer

A PATTERN OF GOOD WORKS

In all things showing yourself to be a pattern of good works;
in doctrine showing integrity, reverence, incorruptibility.
Titus 2:7 NKJV

It has been said that character is what we are when nobody is watching. How true. When we do things that we know aren't right, we try to hide them from our families and friends. But even then, God is watching.

If you sincerely wish to walk with God, you must seek, to the best of your ability, to follow His commandments. When you do, your character will take care of itself . . . and you won't need to look over your shoulder to see who, besides God, is watching.

Often, our character is at greater risk in prosperity than in adversity.

Beth Moore

Here lies the tremendous mystery—that God should be all-powerful, yet refuse to coerce. He summons us to cooperation. We are honored in being given the opportunity to participate in His good deeds. Remember how He asked for help in performing His miracles: Fill the water pots, stretch out your hand, distribute the loaves.

Elisabeth Elliot

A RELATIONSHIP THAT HONORS GOD

I am always praising you; all day long I honor you.

Psalm 71:8 NCV

As you think about the nature of your relationship with God, remember this: you will always have some type of relationship with Him—it is inevitable that your life must be lived in relationship to God. The question is not if you will have a relationship with Him; the burning question is whether or not that relationship will be one that seeks to honor Him.

Are you willing to place God first in your life? And, are you willing to welcome God's Son into your heart? Unless you can honestly answer these questions with a resounding yes, then your relationship with God isn't what it could be or should be. Thankfully, God is always available, He's always ready to forgive, and He's waiting to hear from you now. The rest, of course, is up to you.

———————

The Holy Spirit testifies of Jesus. So when you are filled with the Holy Spirit, you speak about our Lord and really live to His honor.

Corrie ten Boom

A PLACE OF WORSHIP

For where two or three come together in my name, there am I with them.

Matthew 18:20 NIV

In the Book of Acts, Luke reminds us to "feed the church of God" (20:28). As Christians who have been saved by a loving, compassionate Creator, we are compelled not only to worship Him in our hearts but also to worship Him in the presence of fellow believers.

We live in a world that is teeming with temptations and distractions—a world where good and evil struggle in a constant battle to win our hearts and souls. Our challenge, of course, is to ensure that we cast our lot on the side of God. One way to ensure that we do so is by the practice of regular, purposeful worship with our families. When we worship God faithfully and fervently, we are blessed.

The house of God is not a safe place. It is a cross where time and eternity meet, and where we are—or should be—challenged to live more vulnerably, more interdependently.

Madeleine L'Engle

Going to church does not make you a Christian anymore than going to McDonald's makes you a hamburger.

Anonymous

THE ULTIMATE INSTRUCTION MANUAL

He who scorns instruction will pay for it, but he who respects a command is rewarded.

Proverbs 13:13 NIV

The Holy Bible contains thorough instructions which, if followed, lead to fulfillment, righteousness, and salvation. But, if we choose to ignore God's commandments, the results are as predictable as they are tragic.

A righteous life has many components: faith, honesty, generosity, love, kindness, humility, gratitude, and worship, to name but a few. If we seek to follow the steps of our Savior, Jesus Christ, we must seek to live according to His commandments. Let us follow God's commandments, and let us conduct our lives in such a way that we might be shining examples for those who have not yet found Christ.

To yield to God means to belong to God, and to belong to God means to have all His infinite power. To belong to God means to have all.

Hannah Whitall Smith

If we are not continually fed with God's Word, we will starve spiritually.

Stormie Omartian

THE LORD IS NEAR

Draw near to God, and He will draw near to you.
James 4:8 HCSB

Since God is everywhere, we are free to sense His presence whenever we take the time to quiet our souls and turn our prayers to Him. But sometimes, amid the incessant demands of everyday life, we turn our thoughts far from God; when we do, we suffer.

Do you set aside quiet moments each day to offer praise to your Creator? As a woman who has received the gift of God's grace, you most certainly should. Silence is a gift that you give to yourself and to God. During these moments of stillness, you will often sense the infinite love and power of your Creator— and He, in turn, will speak directly to your heart.

The familiar words of Psalm 46:10 remind us to "Be still, and know that I am God." When we do so, we encounter the awesome presence of our loving Heavenly Father, and we are comforted in the knowledge that God is not just near. He is here.

God walks with us. He scoops us up in His arms or simply sits with us in silent strength until we cannot avoid the awesome recognition that yes, even now, He is here.

Gloria Gaither

SEEKING HIS WILL

Teach me to do Your will, for You are my God; Your Spirit is good. Lead me in the land of uprightness.

Psalm 143:10 NKJV

God has a plan for our world and our lives. God does not do things by accident; He is willful and intentional. Unfortunately for us, we cannot always understand the will of God. Why? Because we are mortal beings with limited understanding. Although we cannot fully comprehend the will of God, we should always trust the will of God.

As this day unfolds, seek God's will and obey His Word. When you entrust your life to Him without reservation, He will give you the courage to meet any challenge, the strength to endure any trial, and the wisdom to live in His righteousness and in His peace.

The only safe place is in the center of God's will. It is not only the safest place. It is also the most rewarding and the most satisfying place to be.

Gigi Graham Tchividjian

The purpose of all prayer is to find God's will and to make that will our prayer.

Catherine Marshall

GOOD HABITS, BAD HABITS

Do not be deceived: "Evil company corrupts good habits."

1 Corinthians 15:33 NKJV

It's an old saying and a true one: First, you make your habits, and then your habits make you. Some habits will inevitably bring you closer to God; other habits will lead you away from the path He has chosen for you. If you sincerely desire to improve your spiritual health, you must honestly examine the habits that make up the fabric of your day. And you must abandon those habits that are displeasing to God.

If you trust God, and if you keep asking for His help, He can transform your life. If you sincerely ask Him to help you, the same God who created the universe will help you defeat the harmful habits that have heretofore defeated you. So, if at first you don't succeed, keep praying. God is listening, and He's ready to help you become a better person if you ask Him . . . so ask today.

If you want to form a new habit, get to work. If you want to break a bad habit, get on your knees.

Marie T. Freeman

Prayer is a habit. Worship is a habit. Kindness is a habit. And if you want to please God, you'd better make sure that these habits are your habits.

Marie T. Freeman

DISCOVERING HOPE

These things I have spoken to you, that in Me you may have peace. In the world you will have tribulation; but be of good cheer, I have overcome the world.

John 16:33 NKJV

There are few sadder sights on earth than the sight of a person who has lost all hope. In difficult times, hope can be elusive, but Christians need never lose it. After all, God is good; His love endures; He has promised His children the gift of eternal life.

If you find yourself falling into the spiritual traps of worry and discouragement, consider the words of Jesus. It was Christ who promised, "In the world you will have tribulation; but be of good cheer, I have overcome the world." This world is indeed a place of trials and tribulations, but as believers, we are secure. God has promised us peace, joy, and eternal life. And, of course, God always keeps His promises.

———————

And still today, when you boil it all down, our message to the world—even to the world that comes disguised as our child's schoolteacher, our next-door neighbor, or our personal hair stylist—is hope. Hope beyond the slavery of sin. And hope beyond the grave.

Becky Tirabassi

TO JUDGE OR NOT TO JUDGE

When they continued to ask Jesus their question, he raised up and said, "Anyone here who has never sinned can throw the first stone at her."

John 8:7 NCV

The warning of Matthew 7:1 is clear: "Judge not, that ye be not judged" (KJV). Yet even the most devoted Christians may fall prey to a powerful yet subtle temptation: the temptation to judge others. But as obedient followers of Christ, we are commanded to refrain from such behavior.

As Jesus came upon a young woman who had been condemned by the Pharisees, He spoke not only to the crowd that was gathered there, but also to all generations when He warned, "He that is without sin among you, let him first cast a stone at her" (John 8:7 KJV). Christ's message is clear, and it applies not only to the Pharisees of ancient times, but also to us.

Only Christ can free us from the prison of legalism, and then only if we are willing to be freed.

Madeleine L'Engle

A PRAYER

Dear Lord, sometimes I am quick to judge others. But, You have commanded me not to judge. Keep me mindful, Father, that when I judge others, I am living outside of Your will for my life. You have forgiven me, Lord. Let me forgive others, let me love them, and let me help them . . . without judging them. Amen

NEVER-ENDING LOVE

And God gave us this command: Those who love God must also love their brothers and sisters.

1 John 4:21 NCV

C. S. Lewis observed, "A man's spiritual health is exactly proportional to his love for God." If we are to enjoy the spiritual health that God intends for us, we must praise Him, we must love Him, and we must obey Him.

When we worship God faithfully and obediently, we invite His love into our hearts. When we truly worship God, we allow Him to rule over our days and our lives. In turn, we grow to love God even more deeply as we sense His love for us.

Today, open your heart to the Father. And let your obedience be a fitting response to His never-ending love.

When we develop an authentic love relationship with God, we will not be able to keep Him compartmentalized in "churchy," religious categories.

Beth Moore

As I spent time with God, growing in my knowledge of Him through prayer, Bible Study, obedience, and submission, He would fill my life. And because God is love and because He would fill me, His love would fill me.

Anne Graham Lotz

LIVING RIGHTEOUSLY

Run away from infantile indulgence. Run after mature righteousness—faith, love, peace—joining those who are in honest and serious prayer before God.

2 Timothy 2:22 MSG

A life of righteousness is lived in accordance with God's commandments. A righteous woman strives to be faithful, honest, generous, disciplined, loving, kind, humble, and grateful, to name only a few of the more obvious qualities which are described in God's Word.

If we seek to follow the steps of Jesus, we must seek to live according to His teachings. In short, we must, to the best of our abilities, live according to the principles contained in the Holy Bible. When we do, we become powerful examples to our families and friends of the blessings that God bestows upon righteous women.

We are in desperate need for women of faith who are willing to courageously stand against sin and stand for righteousness.

Susan Hunt

A PRAYER

Dear Lord, when I turn my thoughts away from You and Your Word, I suffer. But when I turn my thoughts, my faith, and my prayers to You, I am safe. Direct my path, Father, and let me discover Your will for me today and every day that I live. Amen

GIVE ME PATIENCE . . . NOW!

Rest in the Lord, and wait patiently for Him.

Psalm 37:7 NKJV

Psalm 37:7 commands us to wait patiently for God. But as busy women in a fast-paced world, many of us find that waiting quietly for God is difficult. Why? Because we are fallible human beings seeking to live according to our own timetables, not God's. In our better moments, we realize that patience is not only a virtue; it is also a commandment from God.

We human beings are impatient by nature. We know what we want, and we know exactly when we want it: NOW! But, God knows better. He has created a world that unfolds according to His plans, not our own. As believers, we must trust His wisdom and His goodness.

God instructs us to be patient in all things. We must be patient with our families, our friends, and our associates. We must also be patient with our Creator as He unfolds His plan for our lives. And that's as it should be. After all, think how patient God has been with us.

If you want to hear God's voice clearly and you are uncertain, then remain in His presence until He changes that uncertainty. Often much can happen during this waiting for the Lord. Sometimes he changes pride into humility; doubt into faith and peace . . . .

Corrie ten Boom

MAINTAINING PERSPECTIVE

It is important to look at things from God's point of view.

1 Corinthians 4:6 MSG

If a temporary loss of perspective has left you worried, exhausted, or both, it's time to readjust your thought patterns. Negative thoughts are habit-forming; thankfully, so are positive ones. With practice, you can form the habit of focusing on God's priorities and your possibilities. When you do, you'll soon discover that you will spend less time fretting about your challenges and more time praising God for His gifts.

When you call upon the Lord and prayerfully seek His will, He will give you wisdom and perspective. When you make God's priorities your priorities, He will direct your steps and calm your fears. So today and every day hereafter, pray for a sense of balance and perspective. And remember: no problems are too big for God—and that includes yours.

The Bible is a remarkable commentary on perspective. Through its divine message, we are brought face to face with issues and tests in daily living and how, by the power of the Holy Spirit, we are enabled to respond positively to them.

Luci Swindoll

A LIFE OF ABUNDANCE

I have come that they may have life, and that they may have it more abundantly.

John 10:10 NKJV

The 10th chapter of John tells us that Christ came to earth so that our lives might be filled with abundance. But what, exactly, did Jesus mean when He promised "life . . . more abundantly"? Was He referring to material possessions or financial wealth? Hardly. Jesus offers a different kind of abundance: a spiritual richness that extends beyond the temporal boundaries of this world. This everlasting abundance is available to all who seek it and claim it. May we, as believers, claim the riches of Christ Jesus every day that we live, and may we share His blessings with all who cross our path.

The gift of God is eternal life, spiritual life, abundant life through faith in Jesus Christ, the Living Word of God.

Anne Graham Lotz

Ultimately things work out best for those who make the best of the way things work out.

Barbara Johnson

IN TIMES OF ADVERSITY

For whatever is born of God overcomes the world. And this is the victory that has overcome the world—our faith.

1 John 5:4 NKJV

All of us face times of adversity. On occasion, we all must endure the disappointments and tragedies that befall believers and nonbelievers alike. The reassuring words of 1 John 5:4 remind us that when we accept God's grace, we overcome the passing hardships of this world by relying upon His strength, His love, and His promise of eternal life.

When we face the inevitable difficulties of life-here-on-earth, God stands ready to protect us. Our responsibility, of course, is to ask Him for protection. When we call upon Him in heartfelt prayer, He will answer—in His own time and according to His own plan—and He will heal us. And while we are waiting for God's plans to unfold and for His healing touch to restore us, we can be comforted in the knowledge that our Creator will can overcome any obstacle, even if we cannot. Let us take God at His word, and let us trust Him.

God always answers us in the depths, never in the shallows of our soul.

Amy Carmichael

OUR ACTIONS AND OUR BELIEFS

As you have therefore received Christ Jesus the Lord, so walk in Him, rooted and built up in Him and established in the faith, as you have been taught, abounding in it with thanksgiving.

Colossians 2:6-7 NKJV

As Christians, we must do our best to make sure that our actions are accurate reflections of our beliefs. Our theology must be demonstrated, not only by our words but, more importantly, by our actions. In short, we should be practical believers, quick to act whenever we see an opportunity to serve God.

We may proclaim our beliefs to our hearts' content, but our proclamations will mean nothing— to others or to ourselves—unless we accompany our words with deeds that match. The sermons that we live are far more compelling than the ones we preach. So remember this: whether you like it or not, your life is an accurate reflection of your creed. If this fact gives you cause for concern, don't bother talking about the changes that you intend to make—make them. And then, when your good deeds speak for themselves—as they most certainly will—don't interrupt.

In the fulfillment of your duties, let your intentions be so pure that you reject from your actions any other motive than the glory of God and the salvation of souls.

Angela Merici

LIFE'S ROADMAP

There's nothing like the written Word of God for showing you the way to salvation through faith in Christ Jesus. Every part of Scripture is God-breathed and useful one way or another, showing us truth, exposing our rebellion, correcting our mistakes, training us to live God's way. Through the Word we are put together and shaped up for the tasks God has for us.

2 Timothy 3:15-17 MSG

God's Word is unlike any other book. The Bible is a roadmap for life here on earth and for life eternal. As Christians, we are called upon to study God's Holy Word, to trust its promises, to follow its commandments, and to share its Good News with the world.

As women who seek to follow in the footsteps of the One from Galilee, we must study the Bible and meditate upon its meaning for our lives. Otherwise, we deprive ourselves of a priceless gift from our Creator. God's Holy Word is, indeed, a life-changing, one-of-a-kind treasure. And, a passing acquaintance with the Good Book is insufficient for Christians who seek to obey God's Word and to understand His will.

The Reference Point for the Christian is the Bible. All values, judgments, and attitudes must be gauged in relationship to this Reference Point.

Ruth Bell Graham

TAKING TIME TO ASK

He granted their request because they trusted in Him.

1 Chronicles 5:20 HCSB

Sometimes, amid the demands and the frustrations of everyday life, we forget to slow ourselves down long enough to talk with God. Instead of turning our thoughts and prayers to Him, we rely upon our own resources. Instead of praying for strength and courage, we seek to manufacture it within ourselves. Instead of asking God for guidance, we depend only upon our own limited wisdom. The results of such behaviors are unfortunate and, on occasion, tragic.

Are you in need? Ask God to sustain you. Are you troubled? Take your worries to Him in prayer. Are you weary? Seek God's strength. In all things great and small, seek God's wisdom and His grace. He hears your prayers, and He will answer. All you must do is ask.

When will we realize that we're not troubling God with our questions and concerns? His heart is open to hear us—his touch nearer than our next thought—as if no one in the world existed but us. Our very personal God wants to hear from us personally.

Gigi Graham Tchividjian

BEYOND OUR REGRETS

All bitterness, anger and wrath, insult and slander must be removed from you, along with all wickedness. And be kind and compassionate to one another, forgiving one another, just as God also forgave you in Christ.

Ephesians 4:31-32 HCSB

Are you mired in the quicksand of bitterness or regret? If so, you are not only disobeying God's Word; you are also wasting your time. The world holds few if any rewards for those who remain angrily focused upon the past. Still, the act of forgiveness is difficult for all but the most saintly men and women.

Being frail, fallible, imperfect human beings, most of us are quick to anger, quick to blame, slow to forgive, and even slower to forget. Yet as Christians, we are commanded to forgive others, just as we, too, have been forgiven.

If there exists even one person—alive or dead—against whom you hold bitter feelings, it's time to forgive. Or, if you are embittered against yourself for some past mistake or shortcoming, it's finally time to forgive yourself and move on. Hatred, bitterness, and regret are not part of God's plan for your life. Forgiveness is.

Grudges are like hand grenades; it is wise to release them before they destroy you.

Barbara Johnson

BLESSINGS FROM ABOVE

I said to myself, "Relax and rest. God has showered you with blessings."

Psalm 116:7 MSG

Psalm 145 makes this promise: "The LORD is gracious and compassionate, slow to anger and rich in love. The LORD is good to all; he has compassion on all he has made" (vv. 8-9 NIV). As God's children, we are blessed beyond measure, but sometimes, as busy women in a demanding world, we are slow to count our gifts and even slower to give thanks to the Giver. Our blessings include life and health, family and friends, freedom and possessions—for starters. And, the gifts we receive from God are multiplied when we share them with others. May we always give thanks to God for our blessings, and may we always demonstrate our gratitude by sharing them.

Jesus intended for us to be overwhelmed by the blessings of regular days. He said it was the reason he had come: "I am come that they might have life, and that they might have it more abundantly."

Gloria Gaither

God is more anxious to bestow His blessings on us than we are to receive them.

St. Augustine

OUR PRICELESS TREASURES

The promise is for you and your children.

Acts 2:39 NASB

We are aware that God has entrusted us with priceless treasures from above—our children. Every child is a glorious gift from the Father. And, with the Father's gift comes profound responsibilities. Thoughtful parents understand the critical importance of raising their children with love, with family, with discipline, and with God.

If you're lucky enough to be a mother, give thanks to God for the gift of your child. Whether you're the mother of a newborn or a seasoned grandmother, remember this: your child—like every child—is a child of God. May you, as a responsible parent, behave accordingly.

Every child born into the world is a new thought of God, an ever-fresh and radiant possibility.

Kate Douglas Wiggin

Children are not so different from kites. Children were created to fly. But, they need wind, the undergirding, and strength that comes from unconditional love, encouragement, and prayer.

Gigi Graham Tchividjian

OUR ULTIMATE SAVIOR

And we have seen and testify that the Father has sent the Son as Savior of the world.

1 John 4:14 NKJV

Hannah Whitall Smith spoke to believers of every generation when she advised, "Keep your face upturned to Christ as the flowers do to the sun. Look, and your soul shall live and grow." How true. When we turn our hearts to Jesus, we receive His blessings, His peace, and His grace.

Christ is the ultimate Savior of mankind and the personal Savior of those who believe in Him. As His servants, we should place Him at the very center of our lives. And, every day that God gives us breath, we should share Christ's love and His message with a world that needs both.

———————

I now know the power of the risen Lord! He lives! The dawn of Easter has broken in my own soul! My night is gone!

Mrs. Charles E. Cowman

Jesus came down from heaven, revealing exactly what God is like, offering eternal life and a personal relationship with God, on the condition of our rebirth—a rebirth made possible through His own death on the cross.

Anne Graham Lotz

CONTAGIOUS FAITH

Whatever you do, work at it with all your heart, as working for the Lord, not for men.

Colossians 3:23 NIV

Genuine, heartfelt Christianity is contagious. If you enjoy a life-altering relationship with God, that relationship will have an impact on others—perhaps a profound impact.

Are you genuinely excited about your faith? And do you make your enthusiasm known to those around you? Or are you a "silent ambassador" for Christ? God's preference is clear: He intends that you stand before others and proclaim your faith.

Does Christ reign over your life? Then share your testimony and your excitement. The world needs both.

Enthusiasm, like the flu, is contagious—we get it from one another.

Barbara Johnson

Faith is nothing more or less than actively trusting God.

Catherine Marshall

A PRAYER

Dear Lord, I know that others are watching the way that I live my life. Help me to be an enthusiastic Christian with a faith that is contagious. Amen

GOD'S VOICE

For this is commendable, if because of conscience toward God one endures grief, suffering wrongfully.

1 Peter 2:19 NKJV

Billy Graham correctly observed, "Most of us follow our conscience as we follow a wheelbarrow. We push it in front of us in the direction we want to go." To do so, of course, is a profound mistake. Yet all of us, on occasion, have failed to listen to the voice that God planted in our hearts, and all of us have suffered the consequences.

God gave you a conscience for a very good reason: to make your path conform to His will. Wise believers make it a practice to listen carefully to that quiet internal voice. Count yourself among that number. When your conscience speaks, listen and learn. In all likelihood, God is trying to get His message through. And in all likelihood, it is a message that you desperately need to hear.

God desires that we become spiritually healthy enough through faith to have a conscience that rightly interprets the work of the Holy Spirit.

Beth Moore

Jesus challenges you and me to keep our focus daily on the cross of His will if we want to be His disciples.

Anne Graham Lotz

GOD CAN HANDLE IT

Do not be afraid or discouraged, for the LORD is the one
who goes before you. He will be with you; he will neither
fail you nor forsake you.

Deuteronomy 31:8 NLT

Life-here-on-earth can be difficult and
discouraging at times. During our darkest moments,
God offers us strength and courage if we turn our
hearts and our prayers to Him.

As believing Christians, we have every reason to
live courageously. After all, the ultimate battle has
already been fought and won on the cross at Calvary.
But sometimes, because we are imperfect human
beings who possess imperfect faith, we fall prey to
fear and doubt. The answer to our fears, of course,
is God.

The next time you find your courage tested to
the limit, remember that God is as near as your next
breath. He is your shield and your strength; He is your
protector and your deliverer. Call upon Him in your
hour of need and then be comforted. Whatever your
challenge, whatever your trouble, God can handle it
. . . and will!

But God wants you to realize that he is tending to
your needs—not just when your helplessness is thick
and tangible—but even in those times when you feel
the most in control.

Cheri Fuller

DURING DARK DAYS

I have heard your prayer, I have seen your tears; surely I will heal you.

2 Kings 20:5 NKJV

The sadness that accompanies any significant loss is an inevitable fact of life. In time, sadness runs its course and gradually abates. Depression, on the other hand, is a physical and emotional condition that is highly treatable.

If you find yourself feeling "blue," perhaps it's a logical reaction to the ups and downs of daily life. But if you or someone close to you have become dangerously depressed, it's time to seek professional help.

Some days are light and happy, and some days are not. When we face the inevitable dark days of life, we must choose how we will respond. Will we allow ourselves to sink even more deeply into our own sadness, or will we do the difficult work of pulling ourselves out? We bring light to the dark days of life by turning first to God, and then to trusted family members, friends, and medical professionals. When we do, the clouds will eventually part, and the sun will shine once more upon our souls.

Emotions we have not poured out in the safe hands of God can turn into feelings of hopelessness and depression. God is safe.

Beth Moore

TODAY'S OPPORTUNITIES

But encourage each other daily, while it is still called today, so that none of you is hardened by sin's deception.
Hebrews 3:13 HCSB

The 118th Psalm reminds us, "This is the day which the Lord hath made; we will rejoice and be glad in it" (v. 24 KJV). As we rejoice in this day that the Lord has given us, let us remember that an important part of today's celebration is the time we spend celebrating others. Each day provides countless opportunities to encourage others and to praise their good works. When we do, we not only spread seeds of joy and happiness, we also follow the commandments of God's Holy Word.

How can we build others up? By celebrating their victories and their accomplishments. So look for the good in others and celebrate the good that you find. When you do, you'll be a powerful force of encouragement in the world . . . and a worthy servant to your God.

Encouragement starts at home, but it should never end there.

Marie T. Freeman

Lovely, complicated wrappings sheath the gift of one-day-more; breathless, I untie the package—never lived this day before!

Gloria Gaither

HUMBLED BY HIS SACRIFICE

But as for me, I will never boast about anything except the cross of our Lord Jesus Christ, through whom the world has been crucified to me, and I to the world.

Galatians 6:14 HCSB

As we consider Christ's sacrifice on the cross, we should be profoundly humbled. And today, as we come to Christ in prayer, we should do so in a spirit of humble devotion.

Christ humbled Himself on a cross—for you. He shed His blood—for you. He has offered to walk with you through this life and throughout all eternity. As you approach Him today in prayer, think about His sacrifice and His grace. And be humble.

The sacrifice of the Lamb is absolutely sufficient in itself to take away our sin and reconcile us to God.

Anne Graham Lotz

To view ourselves through our Creator's loving, tear-filled eyes, we need to climb Calvary's hill and look down from the cross of Christ—for that is where God declared that we are worth the life of His precious Son.

Susan Lenzkes

GOOD PRESSURES, BAD PRESSURES

Do you think I am trying to make people accept me? No, God is the One I am trying to please. Am I trying to please people? If I still wanted to please people, I would not be a servant of Christ.

Galatians 1:10 NCV

Our world is filled with pressures: some good, some bad. The pressures that we feel to follow God's will and obey His commandments are positive pressures. God places them on our hearts, and He intends that we act in accordance with His leadings. But we also face different pressures, ones that are definitely not from God. When we feel pressured to do things—or even to think thoughts—that lead us away from God, we must beware.

Society seeks to mold us into more worldly beings; God seeks to mold us into new beings that are most certainly not conformed to this world. If we are to please God, we must resist the pressures that society seeks to impose upon us, and we must conform ourselves, instead, to God's will, to His path, and to His Son.

True friends will always lift you higher and challenge you to walk in a manner pleasing to our Lord.

Lisa Bevere

It wasn't the apple, it was the pair.

Anonymous

WHEN THE ANSWER IS "NO"

God answered their prayers because they trusted him.
1 Chronicles 5:20 MSG

God answers our prayers. What God does not do is this: He does not always answer our prayers as soon as we might like, and He does not always answer our prayers by saying "Yes." God isn't an order-taker, and He's not some sort of cosmic vending machine. Sometimes—even when we want something very badly—our loving Heavenly Father responds to our requests by saying "No," and we must accept His answer, even if we don't understand it.

God answers prayers not only according to our wishes but also according to His master plan. We cannot know that plan, but we can know the Planner . . . and we must trust His wisdom, His righteousness, and His love. Always.

———————

Let's never forget that some of God's greatest mercies are His refusals. He says no in order that He may, in some way we cannot imagine, say yes. All His ways with us are merciful. His meaning is always love.

Elisabeth Elliot

Surrender to the Lord is not a tremendous sacrifice, not an agonizing performance. It is the most sensible thing you can do.

Corrie ten Boom

SEEKING AND FINDING

Ask, and God will give to you. Search, and you will find.
Knock, and the door will open for you. Yes, everyone who
asks will receive. Everyone who searches will find. And
everyone who knocks will have the door opened.

Matthew 7:7-8 NCV

Where is God? He is everywhere you have ever been and everywhere you will ever go. He is with you night and day; He knows your every thought; He hears your every heartbeat.

Sometimes, in the crush of your daily duties, God may seem far away. Or sometimes, when the disappointments and sorrows of life leave you brokenhearted, God may seem distant, but He is not. When you earnestly seek God, you will find Him because He is here, waiting patiently for you to reach out to Him . . . right here . . . right now.

Our souls were made to live in an upper atmosphere, and we stifle and choke if we live on any lower level. Our eyes were made to look off from these heavenly heights, and our vision is distorted by any lower gazing.

Hannah Whitall Smith

We rarely discover anything monumental about God without discovering something momentous about ourselves. With every revelation comes an invitation to adjust our lives to what we have seen.

Beth Moore

TRUST THE SHEPHERD

The Lord is my shepherd, I shall not want. He makes me lie down in green pastures; He leads me beside quiet waters. He restores my soul.

Psalm 23:1-3 NASB

In the 23rd Psalm, David teaches us that God is like a watchful shepherd caring for His flock. No wonder these verses have provided comfort and hope for generations of believers.

As a busy woman, you know from firsthand experience that life is not always easy. But as a recipient of God's grace, you also know that you are protected by a loving Heavenly Father. On occasion, you will confront circumstances that trouble you to the very core of your soul. When you are afraid, trust in God. When you are worried, turn your concerns over to Him. When you are anxious, be still and listen for the quiet assurance of God's promises. And then, place your life in His hands. He is your Shepherd today and throughout eternity. Trust the Shepherd.

The Lord God of heaven and earth, the Almighty Creator of all things, He who holds the universe in His hand as though it were a very little thing, He is your Shepherd, and He has charged Himself with the care and keeping of you, as a shepherd is charged with the care and keeping of his sheep.

Hannah Whitall Smith

ETERNAL PERSPECTIVE

Our Savior Jesus poured out new life so generously. God's gift has restored our relationship with him and given us back our lives. And there's more life to come—an eternity of life!

Titus 3:6-7 MSG

As mere mortals, our vision for the future, like our lives here on earth, is limited. God's vision is not burdened by such limitations: His plans extend throughout all eternity. Thus, God's plans for you are not limited to the ups and downs of everyday life. Your Heavenly Father has bigger things in mind . . . much bigger things. Christ sacrificed His life on the cross so that we might have eternal life. This gift, freely given by God's only begotten Son, is the priceless possession of everyone who accepts Him as Lord and Savior.

As you struggle with the inevitable hardships and occasional disappointments of everyday life, remember that God has invited you to accept His abundance not only for today but also for all eternity. So keep things in perspective. Although you will inevitably encounter occasional defeats in this world, you'll have all eternity to celebrate the ultimate victory in the next.

The unfolding of our friendship with the Father will be a never-ending revelation stretching on into eternity.

Catherine Marshall

GOD AND FAMILY

Let the Word of Christ—the Message—have the run of the house. Give it plenty of room in your lives.

Colossians 3:16 MSG

These are difficult days for our nation and for our families. But, thankfully, God is bigger than all of our challenges. God loves us and protects us. In times of trouble, He comforts us; in times of sorrow, He dries our tears. When we are troubled or weak or sorrowful, God is as near as our next breath.

Are you concerned for the well-being of your family? You are not alone. We live in a world where temptation and danger seem to lurk on every street corner. Parents and children alike have good reason to be watchful. But, despite the evils of our time, God remains steadfast. Even in these difficult days, no problem is too big for God.

It matters that we should be true to one another, be loyal to what is a family—only a little family in the great Household, but still a family, with family love alive in it and action as a living bond.

Amy Carmichael

Living life with a consistent spiritual walk deeply influences those we love most.

Vonette Bright

BLESSED BEYOND MEASURE

Our prayers for you are always spilling over into thanksgivings. We can't quit thanking God our Father and Jesus our Messiah for you!

Colossians 1:3 MSG

As believing Christians, we are blessed beyond measure. God sent His only Son to die for our sins. And, God has given us the priceless gifts of eternal love and eternal life. We, in turn, are instructed to approach our Heavenly Father with reverence and thanksgiving. But, as busy women caught up in the inevitable demands of everyday life, we sometimes fail to pause and thank our Creator for the countless blessings He has bestowed upon us. When we slow down and express our gratitude to the One who made us, we enrich our own lives and the lives of those around us. Thanksgiving should become a habit, a regular part of our daily routines. Yes, God has blessed us beyond measure, and we owe Him everything, including our eternal praise.

———————

Do we not continually pass by blessings innumerable without notice, and instead fix our eyes on what we feel to be our trials and our losses, and think and talk about these until our whole horizon is filled with them, and we almost begin to think we have no blessings at all?

Hannah Whitall Smith

GENTLENESS OF SPIRIT

Your beauty should not come from outward adornment,
such as braided hair and the wearing of gold jewelry and
fine clothes. Instead, it should be that of your inner self,
the unfading beauty of a gentle and quiet spirit, which is
of great worth in God's sight.

1 Peter 3:3-4 NIV

In a letter to the Christians at Philippi, Paul instructed his friends to make their gentleness evident to all. But, even for the most dedicated Christians, it is sometimes difficult to be gentle. As fallible human beings, we are subject to the normal frustrations of daily life, and when we are, we are tempted to strike out in anger.

As long as you live here on earth, you will face countless opportunities to lose your temper over small, relatively insignificant events: a traffic jam, a spilled cup of coffee, an inconsiderate comment, a broken promise. When you are tempted to lose your temper over the minor inconveniences of life, don't. Turn away from anger and turn instead to God; when you do, He will fill you with a loving spirit that will help you deal gently and generously with others.

This hard place in which you perhaps find yourself is the very place in which God is giving you opportunity to look only to Him, to spend time in prayer, and to learn long-suffering, gentleness, meekness—in short, to learn the depths of the love that Christ Himself has poured out on all of us.

Elisabeth Elliot

THE CHOICE TO FORGIVE

You have heard that it was said, "Love your neighbor and hate your enemy." But I tell you: Love your enemies and pray for those who persecute you.

Matthew 5:43-44 NIV

Forgiveness is a choice. We can either choose to forgive those who have injured us, or not. When we obey God by offering forgiveness to His children, we are blessed. But when we allow bitterness and resentment to poison our hearts, we are tortured by our own shortsightedness.

Do you harbor resentment against anyone? If so, you are faced with an important decision: whether or not to forgive the person who has hurt you. God's instructions are clear: He commands you to forgive. And the time to forgive is now because tomorrow may be too late . . . for you.

God gives us permission to forget our past and the understanding to live our present. He said He will remember our sins no more. (Psalm 103:11-12)

Serita Ann Jakes

Forgiveness is actually the best revenge because it not only sets us free from the person we forgive, but it frees us to move into all that God has in store for us.

Stormie Omartian

THE SEEDS OF GENEROSITY

Freely you have received, freely give.

Matthew 10:8 NIV

Paul reminds us that when we sow the seeds of generosity, we reap bountiful rewards in accordance with God's plan for our lives. Thus, we are instructed to give cheerfully and without reservation: "But this I say, He which soweth sparingly shall reap also sparingly; and he which soweth bountifully shall reap also bountifully. Every man according as he purposeth in his heart, so let him give; not grudgingly, or of necessity: for God loveth a cheerful giver" (2 Corinthians 9:6-7 KJV).

Today, make this pledge and keep it: Be a cheerful, generous, courageous giver. The world needs your help, and you need the spiritual rewards that will be yours when you give it.

As faithful stewards of what we have, ought we not to give earnest thought to our staggering surplus?

Elisabeth Elliot

The measure of a life, after all, is not its duration but its donation.

Corrie ten Boom

TRANSCENDENT LOVE

Who will separate us from the love of Christ? Will tribulation, or distress, or persecution, or famine, or nakedness, or peril, or sword? . . . But in all these things we overwhelmingly conquer through Him who loved us.

Romans 8:35, 37 NASB

Where can we find God's love? Everywhere. God's love transcends space and time. It reaches beyond the heavens, and it touches the darkest, smallest corner of every human heart. When we become passionate in our devotion to the Father, when we sincerely open our minds and hearts to Him, His love does not arrive "some day"—it arrives immediately.

Today, take God at His word and welcome His Son into your heart. When you do, God's transcendent love will surround you and transform you, now and forever.

Praise the Father for his loving kindness; tenderly cares He for His erring children. Praise Him.

Elizabeth R. Charles

There is no pit so deep that God's love is not deeper still.

Corrie ten Boom

LIMITLESS POWER, LIMITLESS LOVE

I pray also that you will have greater understanding in your heart so you will know the hope to which he has called us and that you will know how rich and glorious are the blessings God has promised his holy people. And you will know that God's power is very great for us who believe.

Ephesians 1:18-19 NCV

Because God's power is limitless, it is far beyond the comprehension of mortal minds. Yet even though we cannot fully understand the awesome power of God, we can praise it. When we worship God with faith and assurance, when we place Him at the absolute center of our lives, we invite His love into our hearts. In turn, we grow to love Him more deeply as we sense His love for us. St. Augustine wrote, "I love you, Lord, not doubtingly, but with absolute certainty. Your Word beat upon my heart until I fell in love with you, and now the universe and everything in it tells me to love you."

Let us pray that we, too, will turn our hearts to the Creator, knowing with certainty that His heart has ample room for each of us, and that we, in turn, must make room in our hearts for Him.

Think big, talk big, act big. Because we have a big God.

Kathryn Kuhlman

THY WILL BE DONE

"Father, if it is Your will, take this cup away from Me; nevertheless not My will, but Yours, be done."

Luke 22:42 NKJV

As human beings with limited understanding, we can never fully comprehend the will of God. But as believers in a benevolent God, we must always trust the will of our Heavenly Father.

Before His crucifixion, Jesus went to the Mount of Olives and poured out His heart to God. Jesus knew of the agony that He was destined to endure, but He also knew that God's will must be done. We, like our Savior, face trials that bring fear and trembling to the very depths of our souls, but like Christ, we, too, must ultimately seek God's will, not our own. When we entrust our lives to Him completely and without reservation, He gives us the strength to meet any challenge, the courage to face any trial, and the wisdom to live in His righteousness.

————

The will of God is the most delicious and delightful thing in the universe.

Hannah Whitall Smith

A PRAYER

Dear Lord, You are the Creator of the universe, and I know that Your plan for my life is grander than I can imagine. Let Your purposes be my purposes, and let me trust in the assurance of Your promises. Amen

HAPPINESS AND HOLINESS

Happy are the people who live at your Temple . . . .
Happy are those whose strength comes from you.

Psalm 84:4-5 NKJV

Do you seek happiness, abundance, and contentment? If so, here are some things you should do: Love God and His Son; depend upon God for strength; try, to the best of your abilities, to follow God's will; and strive to obey His Holy Word. When you do these things, you'll discover that happiness goes hand-in-hand with righteousness. The happiest people are not those who rebel against God; the happiest people are those who love God and obey His commandments.

What does life have in store for you? A world full of possibilities (of course it's up to you to seize them), and God's promise of abundance (of course it's up to you to accept it). Your Creator has blessed you beyond measure. Honor Him with your prayers, your words, your deeds, and your joy.

Christ is the secret, the source, the substance, the center, and the circumference of all true and lasting gladness.

Mrs. Charles E. Cowman

YOU ARE BLESSED

I will bless them and the places surrounding my hill. I will send down showers in season; there will be showers of blessings.

Ezekiel 34:26 NIV

If you sat down and began counting your blessings, how long would it take? A very, very long time! Your blessings include life, freedom, family, friends, talents, and possessions, for starters. But, your greatest blessing—a gift that is yours for the asking—is God's gift of salvation through Christ Jesus.

Today, begin making a list of your blessings. You most certainly will not be able to make a complete list, but take a few moments and jot down as many blessings as you can. Then give thanks to the giver of all good things: God. His love for you is eternal, as are His gifts. And it's never too soon—or too late—to offer Him thanks.

Oh! what a Savior, gracious to all, Oh! how His blessings round us fall, gently to comfort, kindly to cheer, sleeping or waking, God is near.

Fanny Crosby

God is the giver, and we are the receivers. And His richest gifts are bestowed not upon those who do the greatest things, but upon those who accept His abundance and His grace.

Hannah Whitall Smith

KNOWLEDGE AND WISDOM

By wisdom a house is built, and through understanding it is established; through knowledge its rooms are filled with rare and beautiful treasures.

Proverbs 24:3-4 NIV

If we are to grow as Christians and as women, we need both knowledge and wisdom. Knowledge is found in textbooks. Wisdom, on the other hand, is found in God's Holy Word and in the carefully-chosen words of loving parents, family members, and friends. Knowledge is an important building block in a well-lived life, and it pays rich dividends both personally and professionally. But, wisdom is even more important because it refashions not only the mind, but also the heart.

A big difference exists between a head full of knowledge and the words of God literally abiding in us.

Beth Moore

Knowledge can be learned, but wisdom must be earned. Wisdom is knowledge . . . lived.

Sheila Walsh

PRIORITIES FOR MARRIAGE AND FAMILY

Their first responsibility is to show godliness at home . . . .
1 Timothy 5:4 NLT

If you're a married woman, you know from personal experience that it takes time to build a strong marriage . . . lots of time. Yet we live in a world where time seems to be an ever-shrinking commodity as we rush from place to place with seldom a moment to spare.

Has the busy pace of life robbed you of sufficient time with your loved ones? If so, it's time to adjust your priorities. And God can help. When you allow God to help you organize your day, you'll soon discover that there is ample time for your spouse and your family. So, as you plan for the day ahead, make God's priorities your priorities. When you do, every other priority will have a tendency to fall neatly into place.

My commitment to my marriage vows places me in an utterly unique and profoundly significant relationship with the most important human being on earth—my spouse.

Joni Eareckson Tada

What can we do to promote world peace? Go home and love your family.

Mother Teresa

THE WISDOM TO OBEY

The world and its desires pass away, but the man who does the will of God lives forever.

1 John 2:17 NIV

Since God created Adam and Eve, we human beings have been rebelling against our Creator. Why? Because we are unwilling to trust God's Word, and we are unwilling to follow His commandments. God has given us a guidebook for righteous living called the Holy Bible. It contains thorough instructions which, if followed, lead to fulfillment, righteousness and salvation. But, if we choose to ignore God's commandments, the results are as predictable as they are tragic.

Talking about God is easy; living by His commandments is considerably harder. But, unless we are willing to abide by God's laws, all of our righteous proclamations ring hollow. How can we best proclaim our love for the Lord? By obeying Him. And, for further instructions, read the manual.

God does not want the forced obedience of slaves. Instead, He covets the voluntary love and obedience of children who love Him for Himself.

Catherine Marshall

God is God. Because He is God, He is worthy of my trust and obedience. I will find rest nowhere but in His holy will, a will that is unspeakably beyond my largest notions of what He is up to.

Elisabeth Elliot

THE INNER VOICE

Let us come near to God with a sincere heart and a sure faith, because we have been made free from a guilty conscience, and our bodies have been washed with pure water.

Hebrews 10:22 NCV

American humorist Josh Billings observed, "Reason often makes mistakes, but conscience never does." How true. Even when we deceive our neighbors, and even when we attempt to deceive ourselves, God has given each of us a conscience, a small, quiet voice that tells us right from wrong.

We must listen to that inner voice . . . or else we must accept the consequences that inevitably befall those who choose to rebel against God.

When we learn to listen to Christ's voice for the details of our daily decisions, we begin to know Him personally.

Catherine Marshall

God desires that we become spiritually healthy enough through faith to have a conscience that rightly interprets the work of the Holy Spirit.

Beth Moore

HOPE FOR THE JOURNEY

Since God assured us, "I'll never let you down, never walk off and leave you," we can boldly quote, God is there, ready to help; I'm fearless no matter what.

Hebrews 13:5-6 MSG

Because we are saved by a risen Christ, we can have hope for the future, no matter how desperate our circumstances may seem. After all, God has promised that we are His throughout eternity. And, He has told us that we must place our hopes in Him.

Today, summon the courage to follow God. Even if the path seems difficult, even if your heart is fearful, trust your Heavenly Father and follow Him. Trust Him with your day and your life. Do His work, care for His children, and share His Good News. Let Him guide your steps. He will not lead you astray.

God knows that the strength that comes from wrestling with our fear will give us wings to fly.

Paula Rinehart

What oxygen is to the lungs, such is hope to the meaning of life.

Emil Brunner

DEALING WITH DISAPPOINTMENT

For we do not want you to be ignorant, brethren, of our trouble which came to us in Asia: that we were burdened beyond measure, above strength, so that we despaired even of life. Yes, we had the sentence of death in ourselves, that we should not trust in ourselves but in God who raises the dead, who delivered us from so great a death, and does deliver us; in whom we trust that He will still deliver us.

2 Corinthians 1:8-10 NKJV

From time to time, all of us face life-altering disappointments that leave us breathless. Oftentimes, these disappointments come unexpectedly, leaving us with more questions than answers. But even when we don't have all the answers—or, for that matter, even when we don't seem to have any of the answers—God does. Whatever our circumstances, whether we stand atop the highest mountain or wander through the darkest valley, God is ready to protect us, to comfort us, and to heal us. Our task is to let Him.

The amazing thing is that God follows us into the blackened ruins of our failed dreams, our misbegotten mirages, into the house of cards that has collapsed on us in some way and he speaks, not with the chastisement we feel we deserve, but of all things, with tenderness.

Paula Rinehart

BEYOND NEGATIVITY

Do not be afraid or discouraged, for the LORD is the one who goes before you. He will be with you; he will neither fail you nor forsake you.

Deuteronomy 31:8 NLT

We Christians have many reasons to celebrate. God is in His heaven; Christ has risen, and we are the sheep of His flock. Yet sometimes, even the most devout Christian women can become discouraged. After all, we live in a world where expectations can be high and demands can be even higher.

If you become discouraged with the direction of your day or your life, turn your thoughts and prayers to God. He is a God of possibility, not negativity. He will help you count your blessings instead of your hardships. And then, with a renewed spirit of optimism and hope, you can properly thank your Father in heaven for His blessings, for His love, and for His Son.

I was learning something important: we are most vulnerable to the piercing winds of doubt when we distance ourselves from the mission and fellowship to which Christ has called us. Our night of discouragement will seem endless and our task impossible, unless we recognize that He stands in our midst.

Joni Eareckson Tada

GETTING IT ALL DONE

Everyone was trying to touch him—so much energy surging from him, so many people healed!

Luke 6:19 MSG

All of us have moments when we feel drained. All of us suffer through difficult days, trying times, and perplexing periods of our lives. During times of hardship, we are tempted to burn the candle at both ends, but we should resist this temptation. Instead, we should strive to place first things first by saying no to the things that we simply don't have the time or the energy to do.

If you're a woman with too many demands and too few hours in which to meet them, don't fret. Instead, focus upon God and upon His love for you. Then, ask Him for the wisdom to prioritize your life and the strength to fulfill your responsibilities. God will give you the energy to do the most important things on today's to-do list . . . if you ask Him. So ask Him.

If choosing to spend time alone with God is a real struggle—a heavy-handed demand that only adds more guilt and stress to your already overblown schedule—it's time to change the way you approach his presence.

Doris Greig

WE ARE ALL ROLE MODELS

We're Christ's representatives. God uses us to persuade men and women to drop their differences and enter into God's work of making things right between them. We're speaking for Christ himself now: Become friends with God; he's already a friend with you.

2 Corinthians 5:20 MSG

Whether we like it or not, all of us are role models. Our friends and family members watch our actions and, as followers of Christ, we are obliged to act accordingly.

What kind of example are you? Are you the kind of woman whose life serves as a genuine example of righteousness? Are you a woman whose behavior serves as a positive role model for young people? Are you the kind of woman whose actions, day in and day out, are based upon kindness, faithfulness, and a love for the Lord? If so, you are not only blessed by God, you are also a powerful force for good in a world that desperately needs positive influences such as yours.

Corrie ten Boom advised, "Don't worry about what you do not understand. Worry about what you do understand in the Bible but do not live by." And that's sound advice because our families and friends are watching . . . and so, for that matter, is God.

We are to leave an impression on all those we meet that communicates whose we are and what kingdom we represent.

Lisa Bevere

ALL IN THE FAMILY

Let the Word of Christ—the Message—have the run of the house. Give it plenty of room in your lives. Instruct and direct one another using good common sense. And sing, sing your hearts out to God! Let every detail in your lives—words, actions, whatever—be done in the name of the Master, Jesus, thanking God the Father every step of the way.

Colossians 3:16-17 MSG

As every woman knows, family life is a mixture of conversations, mediations, irritations, deliberations, commiserations, frustrations, negotiations and celebrations. In other words, the life of the typical woman is incredibly varied.

Certainly, in the life of every family, there are moments of frustration and disappointment. Lots of them. But, for those who are lucky enough to live in the presence of a close-knit, caring clan, the rewards far outweigh the frustrations. That's why we pray fervently for our family members, and that's why we love them despite their faults.

No family is perfect, and neither is yours. But, despite the inevitable challenges and occasional hurt feelings of family life, your clan is God's gift to you. That little band of men, women, kids, and babies is a priceless treasure on temporary loan from the Father above. Give thanks to the Giver for the gift of family . . . and act accordingly.

THE FINANCIAL GUIDE

The blessing of the Lord makes one rich . . . .
Proverbs 10:22 NKJV

God's Word is not only a roadmap to eternal life, it is also an indispensable guidebook for life here on earth. As such, the Bible has much to say about your life and your finances.

God's Word can be a roadmap to a place of righteous and abundance. Make it your roadmap. God's wisdom can be a light to guide your steps. Claim it as your light. God's Word can be an invaluable tool for crafting a better day and a better life. Make it your tool. And finally, God's Word can help you organize your financial life in such a way that you have less need to worry and more time to celebrate His glorious creation. If that sounds appealing, open your Bible, read its instructions, and follow them.

Here's a good recipe for managing your money: Never make a big financial decision without first talking it over with God.

Marie T. Freeman

If the Living Logos of God has the power to create and sustain the universe . . . He is more than able to sustain your marriage and your ministry, your faith and your finances, your hope and your health.

Anne Graham Lotz

LOVE THAT FORGIVES

But when you are praying, first forgive anyone you are holding a grudge against, so that your Father in heaven will forgive your sins, too.

Mark 11:25 NLT

Genuine love is an exercise in forgiveness. If we wish to build lasting relationships, we must learn how to forgive. Why? Because our loved ones are imperfect (as are we). How often must we forgive our family and friends? More times than we can count. Why? Because that's what God wants us to do.

Perhaps granting forgiveness is hard for you. If so, you are not alone. Genuine, lasting forgiveness is often difficult to achieve—difficult but not impossible. Thankfully, with God's help, all things are possible, and that includes forgiveness. But, even though God is willing to help, He expects you to do some of the work. And make no mistake: forgiveness is work, which is okay with God. He knows that the payoffs are worth the effort.

Have you thought that your willingness to forgive is really your affirmation of the power of God to do you good?

Paula Rinehart

God calls upon the loved not just to love but to be loving. God calls upon the forgiven not just to forgive but to be forgiving.

Beth Moore

IN HIS HANDS

Don't brashly announce what you're going to do tomorrow;
you don't know the first thing about tomorrow.

Proverbs 27:1 MSG

The old saying is both familiar and true: "Man proposes and God disposes." Our world unfolds according to God's plans, not our wishes. Thus, boasting about future events is to be avoided by those who acknowledge God's sovereignty over all things.

Are you planning for a better tomorrow for yourself and your family? If so, you are to be congratulated: God rewards forethought in the same way that He often punishes impulsiveness. But as you make your plans, do so with humility, with gratitude, and with trust in your Heavenly Father. His hand directs the future; to think otherwise is both arrogant and naïve.

No matter how heavy the burden, daily strength is given, so I expect we need not give ourselves any concern as to what the outcome will be. We must simply go forward.

Annie Armstrong

Nothing can reach us, from any source in earth or hell, no matter how evil, which God cannot turn to His own redemptive purpose. Let us be glad that the way is not a game of chance—it is a way appointed for God's eternal glory and our final good.

Elisabeth Elliot

GOD IS LOVE

God is love; and he that dwelleth in love dwelleth in God, and God in him.

1 John 4:16 KJV

The Bible makes this promise: God is love. It's a sweeping statement, a profoundly important description of what God is and how God works. God's love is perfect. When we open our hearts to His perfect love, we are touched by the Creator's hand, and we are transformed.

Today, even if you can only carve out a few quiet moments, offer sincere prayers of thanksgiving to your Creator. He loves you now and throughout all eternity. Open your heart to His presence and His love.

———————

Let's never forget that some of God's greatest mercies are His refusals. He says no in order that He may, in some way we cannot imagine, say yes. All His ways with us are merciful. His meaning is always love.

Elisabeth Elliot

Accepting God's love as a gift instead of trying to earn it had somehow seemed presumptuous and arrogant to me, when, in fact, my pride was tricking me into thinking that I could merit His love and forgiveness with my own strength.

Lisa Whelchel

TRUST HIM TO GUIDE YOU

Trust the Lord your God with all your heart and lean not on your own understanding; in all your ways acknowledge him, and he will make your paths straight.

Proverbs 3:5-6 NIV

As Christians whose salvation has been purchased by the blood of Christ, we have every reason to live joyously and courageously. After all, Christ has already fought and won our battle for us—He did so on the cross at Calvary. But despite Christ's sacrifice, and despite God's promises, we may become confused or disoriented by the endless complications and countless distractions of life.

If you're unsure of your next step, lean upon God's promises and lift your prayers to Him. Remember that God is your protector. Open yourself to His heart, and trust Him to guide you. When you do, God will direct your steps, and you will receive His blessings today, tomorrow, and throughout eternity.

––––––––––

It is a joy that God never abandons His children. He guides faithfully all who listen to His directions.

Corrie ten Boom

A PRAYER

Dear Lord, today I will trust You more completely. I will lean upon Your understanding, not mine. And I will trust You to guide my steps along a path of Your choosing. Amen

ULTIMATE PROTECTION

God is striding ahead of you. He's right there with you.
He won't let you down; he won't leave you. Don't be
intimidated. Don't worry.

Deuteronomy 31:8 MSG

God has promised to protect us, and He intends
to fulfill His promise. In a world filled with dangers
and temptations, God is the ultimate armor. In a
world filled with misleading messages, God's Word
is the ultimate truth. In a world filled with more
frustrations than we can count, God's Son offers the
ultimate peace.

Will you accept God's peace and wear God's
armor against the dangers of our world? Hopefully
so, because when you do, you can live courageously,
knowing that you possess the ultimate protection:
God's unfailing love for you.

Our future may look fearfully intimidating, yet we can
look up to the Engineer of the Universe, confident
that nothing escapes His attention or slips out of the
control of those strong hands.

Elisabeth Elliot

He goes before us, follows behind us, and hems us safe
inside the realm of His protection.

Beth Moore

SEEKING GOD
AND FINDING HAPPINESS

But happy are those . . . whose hope is in the LORD their God.

Psalm 146:5 NLT

Happiness depends less upon our circumstances than upon our thoughts. When we turn our thoughts to God, to His gifts, and to His glorious creation, we experience the joy that God intends for His children. But, when we focus on the negative aspects of life, we suffer needlessly.

Do you sincerely want to be a happy Christian? Then set your mind and your heart upon God's love and His grace. The fullness of life in Christ is available to all who seek it and claim it. Count yourself among that number. Seek first the salvation that is available through a personal relationship with Jesus Christ, and then claim the joy, the peace, and the spiritual abundance that the Shepherd offers His sheep.

We will never be happy until we make God the source of our fulfillment and the answer to our longings.

Stormie Omartian

I am convinced beyond a shadow of any doubt that the most valuable pursuit we can embark upon is to know God.

Kay Arthur

HIS HEALING TOUCH

I am the Lord that healeth thee.

Exodus 15:26 KJV

Are you concerned about your spiritual, physical, or emotional health? If so, there is a timeless source of comfort and assurance that is as near as your bookshelf. That source is the Holy Bible.

God's Word has much to say about every aspect of your life, including your health. And, when you face concerns of any sort—including health-related challenges—God is with you. So trust your medical doctor to do his or her part, but place your ultimate trust in your benevolent Heavenly Father. His healing touch, like His love, endures forever.

Jesus Christ is the One by Whom, for Whom, through Whom everything was made. Therefore, He knows what's wrong in your life and how to fix it.

Anne Graham Lotz

If you want to receive emotional healing from God and come into an area of wholeness, you must realize that healing is a process, and you must allow the Lord to deal with you and your problem in His own way and in His own time.

Joyce Meyer

SELF-MADE?

Respecting the Lord and not being proud will bring you wealth, honor, and life.

Proverbs 22:4 NCV

We have heard it said on countless occasions: "He's a self-made man," or "She's a self-made woman." In truth, none of us are self-made. We all owe countless debts that we can never repay. Our first debt, of course, is to our Father in heaven—who has given us everything that we are and will ever be—and to His Son who sacrificed His own life so that we might live eternally. We are also indebted to ancestors, parents, teachers, friends, spouses, family members, coworkers, fellow believers . . . and the list, of course, goes on.

Most of us, it seems, are more than willing to stick out our chests and say, "Look at me; I did that!" But in our better moments, in the quiet moments when we search the depths of our own hearts, we know better. Whatever "it" is, God did that. And He deserves the credit.

As children observe an attitude and spirit of humility in us, our example will pave the way for them when they must admit to their Heavenly Father their own desperate need for guidance and forgiveness.

Annie Chapman

LOVE IS A CHOICE

Beloved, if God so loved us, we also ought to love one another.

1 John 4:11 NASB

Love is always a choice. Sometimes, of course, we may "fall in love," but it takes work to stay there. Sometimes, we may be "swept off our feet," but the "sweeping" is only temporary; sooner or later, if love is to endure, one must plant one's feet firmly on the ground. The decision to love another person for a lifetime is much more than the simple process of "falling in" or "being swept up." It requires "reaching out," "holding firm," and "lifting up." Love, then, becomes a decision to honor and care for the other person, come what may.

A soul cannot live without loving. It must have something to love, for it was created to love.

Catherine of Siena

A PRAYER

Dear Lord, You have given me the gift of love; let me share that gift with others. And, keep me mindful that the essence of love is not to receive it, but to give it, today and forever. Amen

BEYOND MATERIALISM

And how do you benefit if you gain the whole world but lose your own soul in the process? Is anything worth more than your soul?

Mark 8:36-37 NLT

In our modern society, we need money to live. But as Christians, we must never make the acquisition of money the central focus of our lives. Money is a tool, but it should never overwhelm our sensibilities. The focus of life must be squarely on things spiritual, not things material.

Whenever we place our love for material possessions above our love for God—or when we yield to the countless other temptations of everyday living—we find ourselves engaged in a struggle between good and evil. Let us respond to this struggle by freeing ourselves from that subtle yet powerful temptation: the temptation to love the world more than we love God.

We are made spiritually lethargic by a steady diet of materialism.

Mary Morrison Suggs

Why is love of gold more potent than love of souls?

Lottie Moon

BLESSED OBEDIENCE

When you and your children return to the LORD your God and obey him with all your heart and with all your soul according to everything I command you today, then the LORD your God will restore your fortunes and have compassion on you and gather you again from all the nations where he scattered you.

Deuteronomy 30:2-3 NIV

We live in a world filled with temptations, distractions, and countless opportunities to disobey God. But as women who seek to be godly role models for our families, we must turn our thoughts and our hearts away from the evils of this world. We must turn instead to God.

Talking about God is easy; living by His laws is considerably harder. But unless we are willing to live obediently, all our righteous words ring hollow.

How can we best proclaim our love for the Lord? By obeying Him. We must seek God's counsel and trust the counsel He gives. And, when we invite God into our hearts and live according to His commandments, we are blessed today and tomorrow and forever.

God is God. Because He is God, He is worthy of my trust and obedience. I will find rest nowhere but in His holy will, a will that is unspeakably beyond my largest notions of what He is up to.

Elisabeth Elliot

LOST IN THE CROWD

The fear of human opinion disables; trusting in God protects you from that.

Proverbs 29:25 MSG

Rick Warren observed, "Those who follow the crowd usually get lost in it." We know these words to be true, but oftentimes we fail to live by them. Instead of trusting God for guidance, we imitate our neighbors and suffer the consequences. Instead of seeking to please our Father in heaven, we strive to please our peers, with decidedly mixed results.

Whom will you try to please today: your God or your associates? Your obligation is most certainly not to neighbors, to friends, or even to family members. Your obligation is to an all-knowing, all-powerful God. You must seek to please Him first and always. No exceptions.

It is comfortable to know that we are responsible to God and not to man. It is a small matter to be judged of man's judgement.

Lottie Moon

If you choose to awaken a passion for God, you will have to choose your friends wisely.

Lisa Bevere

FOOLISH PRIDE

When you do things, do not let selfishness or pride be your guide. Instead, be humble and give more honor to others than to yourselves.

Philippians 2:3 NCV

Sometimes our faith is tested more by prosperity than by adversity. Why? Because in times of plenty, we are tempted to stick out our chests and say, "I did that." But nothing could be further from the truth. All of our blessings start and end with God, and whatever "it" is, He did it. And He deserves the credit.

Who are the greatest among us? Are they the proud and the powerful? Hardly. The greatest among us are the humble servants who care less for their own glory and more for God's glory. If we seek greatness in God's eyes, we must forever praise God's good works, not our own.

When we look at the individual parts of our lives, some things appear unfair and unpleasant. When we take them out of the context of the big picture, we easily drift into the attitude that we deserve better, and the tumble down into the pit of pride begins.

Susan Hunt

SERVING OTHERS WITH LOVE

Whoever wants to become great among you must serve the rest of you like a servant.

Matthew 20:26 NCV

Jesus came to earth as a servant of man and the Savior of mankind. One way that we can demonstrate our love for the Savior is by obeying His commandment to serve one another.

Whom will you choose to serve today? Will you be a woman who cheerfully meets the needs of family and friends? And, will you meet those needs with love in your heart and encouragement on your lips? As you plan for the day ahead, remember that the needs are great and the workers are few. And remember that God is doing His very best to enlist able-bodied believers—like you.

We can love Jesus in the hungry, the naked, and the destitute who are dying . . . If you love, you will be willing to serve. And you will find Jesus in the distressing disguise of the poor.

Mother Teresa

Love is an attribute of God. To love others is evidence of a genuine faith.

Kay Arthur

SETBACKS

And my God shall supply all your need according to His riches in glory by Christ Jesus.

Philippians 4:19 NKJV

All of us experience adversity, disappointments, and hardship. Sometimes we bring these hardships upon ourselves, and sometimes we are victimized by circumstances that we cannot control and cannot fully understand. As human beings with limited insight, we can never completely comprehend the will of our Father in heaven. But as believers in a benevolent God, we must always trust His providence.

Have you been touched by a personal tragedy that you did not deserve and cannot understand? If so, it's time to make peace with life. It's time to forgive others, and, if necessary, to forgive yourself. It's time to accept the unchangeable past, to embrace the priceless present, and to have faith in the promise of tomorrow. It's time to trust God completely. And it's time to reclaim the peace—His peace—that can and should be yours.

———

Measure the size of the obstacles against the size of God.

Beth Moore

BEYOND WORRY

Let not your heart be troubled; you believe in God, believe also in Me.

John 14:1 NKJV

Because we are fallible human beings, we worry. Even though we, as Christians, have the promise of God's love and protection, we find ourselves fretting over the countless details of everyday life.

If you are like most women, you may, on occasion, find yourself worrying about health, about finances, about safety, about relationships, about family, and about countless other challenges of life, some great and some small. Where is the best place to take your worries? Take them to God. Take your troubles to Him, and your fears and your sorrows. And remember: God is trustworthy . . . and you are protected.

Worry is a cycle of inefficient thoughts whirling around a center of fear.

Corrie ten Boom

Submit each day to God, knowing that He is God over all your tomorrows.

Kay Arthur

IT'S UP TO YOU TO ASK

If you need wisdom—if you want to know what God wants you to do—ask him, and he will gladly tell you. He will not resent your asking.

James 1:5 NLT

Jesus made it clear to His disciples: they should petition God to meet their needs. So should we. Genuine, heartfelt prayer produces powerful changes in us and in our world. When we lift our hearts to God, we open ourselves to a never-ending source of divine wisdom and infinite love.

Do you have questions about your future that you simply can't answer? Do you have needs that you simply can't meet by yourself? Do you sincerely seek to know God's unfolding plans for your life? If so, ask Him for direction, for protection, and for strength—and then keep asking Him every day that you live. Whatever your need, no matter how great or small, pray about it and never lose hope. God is not just near; He is here, and He's perfectly capable of answering your prayers. Now, it's up to you to ask.

When trials come your way—as inevitably they will—do not run away. Run to your God and Father.

Kay Arthur

A PRICELESS GIFT

Man shall not live by bread alone, but by every word that proceeds from the mouth of God.

Matthew 4:4 NKJV

The Bible is a priceless gift, a tool for Christians to use as they share the Good News of their Savior, Christ Jesus. Too many Christians, however, keep their spiritual tool kits tightly closed and out of sight.

Jonathan Edwards advised, "Be assiduous in reading the Holy Scriptures. This is the fountain whence all knowledge in divinity must be derived. Therefore let not this treasure lie by you neglected."

God's Holy Word is, indeed, a priceless, one-of-a-kind treasure. Handle it with care, but more importantly, handle it every day . . . starting today.

When we let God's Word seep into our own lives little by little, it nourishes us and becomes part of us.

Janette Oke

Either God's Word keeps you from sin, or sin keeps you from God's Word.

Corrie ten Boom

BORN AGAIN

You have been born again, and this new life did not come from something that dies, but from something that cannot die. You were born again through God's living message that continues forever.

1 Peter 1:23 NCV

Why did Christ die on the cross? Christ sacrificed His life so that we might be born again. This gift, freely given from God's only begotten Son, is the priceless possession of everyone who accepts Him as Lord and Savior. Let us claim Christ's gift today. Let us walk with the Savior, let us love Him, let us praise Him, and let us share His message of salvation with all those who cross our paths.

The comforting words of Ephesians 2:8 make God's promise clear: "For by grace you have been saved through faith, and that not of yourselves; it is the gift of God" (NKJV). Thus, we are saved not because of our good deeds but because of our faith in Christ. May we, who have been given so much, praise our Savior for the gift of salvation, and may we share the joyous news of our Master's limitless love with our families, with our friends, and with the world.

Being born again is God's solution to our need for love and life and light.

Anne Graham Lotz

LIFE'S FOUNDATION

A wife of noble character who can find? She is worth far more than rubies.

Proverbs 31:10 NIV

Wise women understand that character is a crucial building block in the foundation of a well-lived life. Character is built slowly over a lifetime. It is the sum of every right decision, every honest word, every noble thought, and every heartfelt prayer. It is forged on the anvil of honorable work and polished by the twin virtues of generosity and humility. Character is a precious thing—difficult to build, but easy to tear down; godly women value it and protect it at all costs.

Character cannot be developed in ease and quiet. Only through experience of trial and suffering can the soul be strengthened, vision cleared, ambition inspired, and success achieved.

Helen Keller

Each one of us is God's special work of art. Through us, He teaches and inspires, delights and encourages, informs and uplifts all those who view our lives. God, the master artist, is most concerned about expressing Himself—His thoughts and His intentions—through what He paints in our characters.

Joni Eareckson Tada

GOD IS HERE

Draw near to God, and He will draw near to you.
James 4:8 HCSB

God is constantly making Himself available to you; therefore, when you approach Him obediently and sincerely, You will most certainly find Him: God is always available to you. Whenever it seems to you that God is distant, disinterested, or altogether absent, you may rest assured that your feelings are a reflection of your own emotional state, not an indication of God's absence.

If, during life's darker days, you seek to establish a closer relationship with Him, you can do so because God is not just near, He is here.

Let us preach you, Dear Jesus, without preaching, not by words but by our example, by the casting force, the sympathetic influence of what we do, the evident fullness of the love our hearts bear to you. Amen.

Mother Teresa

God accompanies his children into exile. No space is devoid of God. God is everywhere, even in suffering and in the very heart of punishment. What happens to us touches God. What happens to him concerns us.

Elie Wiesel

SUPPORTING HIS CHURCH

For we are God's fellow workers; you are God's field, you are God's building.

1 Corinthians 3:9 NKJV

The church belongs to God; it is His just as certainly as we are His. When we help build God's church, we bear witness to the changes that He has made in our lives.

Today and every day, let us worship God with grateful hearts and helping hands as we support the church that He has created. Let us witness to our friends, to our families, and to the world. When we do so, we bless others—and we are blessed by the One who sent His Son to die so that we might have eternal life.

The church needs the power and the gifts of the Holy Spirit more now than ever before.

Corrie ten Boom

The house of God is not a safe place. It is a cross where time and eternity meet, and where we are—or should be—challenged to live more vulnerably, more interdependently.

Madeleine L'Engle

A CLEAR CONSCIENCE

If then you were raised with Christ, seek those things which are above, where Christ is, sitting at the right hand of God. Set your mind on things above, not on things on the earth.

Colossians 3:1-2 NKJV

Few things in life torment us more than a guilty conscience. And, few things in life provide more contentment than the knowledge that we are obeying God's commandments.

A clear conscience is one of the rewards we earn when we obey God's Word and follow His will. When we follow God's will and accept His gift of salvation, our earthly rewards are never-ceasing, and our heavenly rewards are everlasting.

Whatever weakens your reason, impairs the tenderness of your conscience, obscures your sense of God, or removes your relish for spiritual things—that is sin to you.

Susanna Wesley

There is no pillow so soft as a clear conscience.

French Proverb

THE MORNING WATCH

Every morning he wakes me. He teaches me to listen like a student. The Lord God helps me learn . . .

Isaiah 50:4-5 NCV

Each new day is a gift from God, and if you are wise, you will spend a few quiet moments each morning thanking the Giver. When you begin each day with your head bowed and your heart lifted, you are reminded of God's love, His protection, and His commandments. Then, you can align your priorities for the coming day with the teachings and commandments that God has placed upon your heart.

So, if you've acquired the unfortunate habit of trying to "squeeze" God into the corners of your life, it's time to reshuffle the items on your to-do list by placing God first. And if you haven't already done so, form the habit of spending quality time with your Father in heaven. He deserves it . . . and so do you.

———————

How motivating it has been for me to view my early morning devotions as time of retreat alone with Jesus, Who desires that I "come with Him by myself to a quiet place" in order to pray, read His Word, listen for His voice, and be renewed in my spirit.

Anne Graham Lotz

WHEN PEOPLE MISBEHAVE

Bad temper is contagious—don't get infected.

Proverbs 22:25 MSG

Face it: sometimes people can be rude . . . very rude. When other people are unkind to you, you may be tempted to strike back, either verbally or in some other way. Don't do it! Instead, remember that God corrects other people's behaviors in His own way, and He doesn't need your help (even if you're totally convinced that He does).

So, when other people behave cruelly, foolishly, or impulsively—as they will from time to time—don't be hotheaded. Instead, speak up for yourself as politely as you can, and walk away. Then, forgive everybody as quickly as you can, and leave the rest up to God.

―――――――――

You can be sure you are abiding in Christ if you are able to have a Christlike love toward the people that irritate you the most.

Vonette Bright

If you can't seem to forgive someone, pray for that person and keep praying for him or her until, with God's help, you've removed the poison of bitterness from your heart.

Marie T. Freeman

TEACHING DISCIPLINE

Whoever accepts correction is on the way to life, but whoever ignores correction will lead others away from life.

Proverbs 10:17 NCV

Wise women understand the importance of discipline. In Proverbs 28:19, God's message is clear: "He who works his land will have abundant food, but the one who chases fantasies will have his fill of poverty" (NIV). When we work diligently and consistently, we can expect a bountiful harvest. But we must never expect the harvest to precede the labor.

Thoughtful Christians understand that God doesn't reward laziness or misbehavior. To the contrary, God expects His children (of all ages) to lead disciplined lives . . . very disciplined lives.

There is no influence so powerful as that of a mother.

Sarah J. Hale

The goal of any discipline is to result in greater freedom.

Anonymous

HOPE IS CONTAGIOUS

*Finally, all of you be of one mind, having compassion
for one another; love as brothers, be tenderhearted, be
courteous.*

1 Peter 3:8 NKJV

One of the reasons that God placed you here
on earth is so that you might become a beacon of
encouragement to the world. As a faithful follower
of the One from Galilee, you have every reason to
be hopeful, and you have every reason to share your
hopes with others. When you do, you will discover that
hope, like other human emotions, is contagious.

As a follower of Christ, you are instructed to
choose your words carefully so as to build others
up through wholesome, honest encouragement
(Ephesians 4:29). So look for the good in others
and celebrate the good that you find. As the old
saying goes, "When someone does something good,
applaud—you'll make two people happy."

One of the ways God refills us after failure is through
the blessing of Christian fellowship. Just experiencing
the joy of simple activities shared with other children
of God can have a healing effect on us.

Anne Graham Lotz

A POSITIVE INFLUENCE

Be an example to the believers in word, in conduct, in love, in spirit, in faith, in purity.

1 Timothy 4:12 NKJV

As followers of Christ, we must each ask ourselves an important question: "What kind of example am I?" The answer to that question determines, in large part, whether or not we are positive influences on our own little corners of the world.

Are you the kind of woman whose life serves as a powerful example of righteousness? Are you a person whose behavior serves as a positive role model for young people? Are you the kind of Christian whose actions, day in and day out, are based upon integrity, fidelity, and a love for the Lord? If so, you are not only blessed by God, you are also a powerful force for good in a world that desperately needs positive influences such as yours.

Let us preach you, Dear Jesus, without preaching, not by words but by our example, by the casting force, the sympathetic influence of what we do, the evident fullness of the love our hearts bear to you. Amen.

Mother Teresa

CARING FOR YOUR FAMILY

But if anyone does not provide for his own, and especially
for those of his household, he has denied the faith and is
worse than an unbeliever.

1 Timothy 5:8 NASB

The words of 1 Timothy 5:8 are unambiguous: if God has blessed us with families, then He expects us to care for them. Sometimes, this profound responsibility seems daunting. And sometimes, even for the most dedicated Christian men, family life holds moments of frustration and disappointment. But, for those who are lucky enough to live in the presence of a close-knit, caring clan, the rewards far outweigh the demands.

No family is perfect, and neither is yours. Despite the inevitable challenges of providing for your family, and despite the occasional hurt feelings of family life, your clan is God's gift to you. Give thanks to the Giver for the gift of family . . . and act accordingly.

When God asks someone to do something for Him entailing sacrifice, He makes up for it in surprising ways. Though He has led Bill all over the world to preach the gospel, He has not forgotten the little family in the mountains of North Carolina.

Ruth Bell Graham

PASS IT ON

Do not neglect the spiritual gift that is within you . . . .
1 Timothy 4:14 NASB

God has given you an array of talents, and He has given you unique opportunities to share those talents with the world. Your Creator intends for you to use your talents for the glory of His kingdom in the service of His children. Will you honor Him by sharing His gifts? And, will you share His gifts humbly and lovingly? Hopefully you will.

The old saying is both familiar and true: "What you are is God's gift to you; what you become is your gift to God." As a woman who has been touched by the transforming love of Jesus Christ, your obligation is clear: You must strive to make the most of your own God-given talents, and you must encourage your family and friends to do likewise. So, make this promise to yourself and to God: Promise to use your talents to minister to your family, to your friends, and to the world. And remember: The best way to say "Thank You" for God's gifts is to use them.

Christian women are often blocked from maximizing their potential because they do not understand the power of the Holy Spirit within them. Many Christian women struggle with the I'm-not-good-enough-smart-enough-talented-enough syndrome. A leader of women understands that every daughter of the King has been uniquely designed and equipped for a purpose.

Susan Hunt

LETTING GO

Those who show mercy to others are happy, because God will show mercy to them.

Matthew 5:7 NCV

Even the most mild-mannered women will, on occasion, have reason to become angry with the inevitable shortcomings of family members and friends. But wise women are quick to forgive others, just as God has forgiven them. The commandment to forgive others is clearly a part of God's Word, but oh how difficult a commandment it can be to follow. Because we are imperfect beings, we are quick to anger, quick to blame, slow to forgive, and even slower to forget. No matter. Even when forgiveness is difficult, God's instructions are straightforward: As Christians who have received the gift of forgiveness, we must now share that gift with others.

Bitterness and regret are not part of God's plan for your life. Forgiveness is. And once you've forgiven others, you can then turn your thoughts to a far more pleasant subject: the incredibly bright future that God has promised.

God expects us to forgive others as He has forgiven us; we are to follow His example by having a forgiving heart.

Vonette Bright

RICHLY BLESSED

God loves a cheerful giver.

2 Corinthians 9:7 NIV

God's Word commands us to be generous, compassionate servants to those who need our support. As believers, we have been richly blessed by our Creator. We, in turn, are called to share our gifts, our possessions, our testimonies, and our talents.

The theme of generosity is one of the cornerstones of Christ's teachings. If we are to be disciples of Christ, we, too, must be cheerful, generous, courageous givers. Our Savior expects no less from us. And He deserves no less.

A cheerful giver does not count the cost of what he gives. His heart is set on pleasing and cheering him to whom the gift is given.

Juliana of Norwich

We do not need to beg Him to bless us; He simply cannot help it.

Hannah Whitall Smith

A PRAYER

Lord, You loved me before I was ever born; You sent Your Son Jesus to redeem me from my sins; You have given me the gift of eternal life. Today, I will share the priceless blessings that I have received: I will share my joy, my possessions, and my faith with others. Amen

HEARING THE CALL

One thing I do, forgetting those things which are behind and reaching forward to those things which are ahead, I press toward the goal for the prize of the upward call of God in Christ Jesus.

Philippians 3:13-14 NKJV

It is vitally important that you heed God's call. In John 15:16, Jesus says, "You did not choose me, but I chose you and appointed you to go and bear fruit—fruit that will last" (NIV). In other words, you have been called by Christ, and now, it is up to you to decide precisely how you will answer.

Have you already found your special calling? If so, you're a very lucky woman. If not, keep searching and keep praying until you discover it. And remember this: God has important work for you to do—work that no one else on earth can accomplish but you.

If God has called you, do not spend time looking over your shoulder to see who is following you.

Corrie ten Boom

A PRAYER

Heavenly Father, You have called me, and I acknowledge that calling. In these quiet moments before this busy day unfolds, I come to You. I will study Your Word and seek Your guidance. Give me the wisdom to know Your will for my life and the courage to follow wherever You may lead me, today and forever. Amen

GOD IS LOVE

He who does not love does not know God, for God is love.

1 John 4:8 NKJV

God loves you. He loves you more than you can imagine; His affection is deeper than you can fathom. God made you in His own image and gave you salvation through the person of His Son Jesus Christ. And as a result, you have an important decision to make. You must decide what to do about God's love: you can return it . . . or not.

When you accept the love that flows from the heart of God, you are transformed. When you embrace God's love, you feel differently about yourself, your neighbors, your community, your church, and your world. When you open your heart to God's love, you will feel compelled to share God's message— and His compassion—with others. God's heart is overflowing—accept His love; return His love; and share His love. Today.

Life in God is a great big hug that lasts forever!

Barbara Johnson

As we focus on His love and Word, in time He will fill our void and loneliness, and He will heal our pain.

Anita Corrine Donihue

SUFFICIENT FOR YOUR NEEDS

And God is able to make all grace abound toward you,
that you, always having all sufficiency in all things, may
have an abundance for every good work.

2 Corinthians 9:8 NKJV

Of this you can be sure: the love of God is sufficient to meet your needs. Whatever dangers you may face, whatever heartbreaks you must endure, God is with you, and He stands ready to comfort you and to heal you.

The Psalmist writes, "Weeping may endure for a night, but joy comes in the morning" (Psalm 30:5 NKJV). But when we are suffering, the morning may seem very far away. It is not. God promises that He is "near to those who have a broken heart" (Psalm 34:18 NKJV).

If you are experiencing the intense pain of a recent loss, or if you are still mourning a loss from long ago, perhaps you are now ready to begin the next stage of your journey with God. If so, be mindful of this fact: the loving heart of God is sufficient to meet any challenge, including yours.

God's all-sufficiency is a major. Your inability is a minor. Major in majors, not in minors.

Corrie ten Boom

WHEN IT'S HARD TO BE KIND

Don't be obsessed with getting your own advantage. Forget yourselves long enough to lend a helping hand.

Philippians 2:4 MSG

Sometimes, when we feel happy or generous, we find it easy to be kind. Other times, when we are discouraged or tired, we can scarcely summon the energy to utter a single kind word. But, God's commandment is clear: He intends that we make the conscious choice to treat others with kindness and respect, no matter our circumstances, no matter our emotions.

Today, as you consider all the things that Christ has done in your life, honor Him by following His commandment and obeying the Golden Rule.

The Golden Rule starts at home, but it should never stop there.

Marie T. Freeman

As you're rushing through life, take time to stop a moment, look into people's eyes, say something kind, and try to make them laugh!

Barbara Johnson

PRIORITIES . . . MOMENT BY MOMENT

You can't go wrong when you love others. When you add up everything in the law code, the sum total is love. But make sure that you don't get so absorbed and exhausted in taking care of all your day-by-day obligations that you lose track of the time and doze off, oblivious to God.

Romans 13:10-11 MSG

Each waking moment holds the potential to think a creative thought or offer a heartfelt prayer. So even if you're a person with too many demands and too few hours in which to meet them, don't panic. Instead, be comforted in the knowledge that when you sincerely seek to discover God's priorities for your life, He will provide answers in marvelous and surprising ways.

Remember: this is the day that God has made and that He has filled it with countless opportunities to love, to serve, and to seek His guidance. Seize those opportunities. And as a gift to yourself, to your family, and to the world, slow down and claim the inner peace that is your spiritual birthright: the peace of Jesus Christ. It is yours for the asking. So ask . . . and be thankful.

In our tense, uptight society where folks are rushing to make appointments they have already missed, a good laugh can be a refreshing as a cup of cold water in the desert.

Barbara Johnson

THE WISDOM TO BE HUMBLE

Don't be selfish; don't live to make a good impression on others.

Philippians 2:3 NLT

God's Word clearly instructs us to be humble. And that's good because, as fallible human beings, we have so very much to be humble about! Yet some of us continue to puff ourselves up, seeming to say, "Look at me!" To do so is wrong.

As Christians, we have been refashioned and saved by Jesus Christ, and that salvation came not because of our own good works but because of God's grace. How, then, can we be prideful? The answer, of course, is that, if we are honest with ourselves and with our God, we simply can't be boastful . . . we must, instead, be eternally grateful and exceedingly humble. The good things in our lives, including our loved ones, come from God. He deserves the credit— and we deserve the glorious experience of giving it to Him.

———————

I have learned that the more we understand how very much God loves us, and the more we comprehend the grace He has demonstrated toward us, the more humble we become.

Serita Ann Jakes

BEING PATIENT
WITH OURSELVES

Knowing God leads to self-control. Self-control leads to patient endurance, and patient endurance leads to godliness.

2 Peter 1:6 NLT

Being patient with other people can be difficult. But sometimes, we find it even more difficult to be patient with ourselves. We have high expectations and lofty goals. We want to accomplish things now, not later. And, of course, we want our lives to unfold according to our own timetables, not God's.

Throughout the Bible, we are instructed that patience is the companion of wisdom. God's message, then, is clear: we must be patient with all people, beginning with that particular person who stares back at us each time we gaze into the mirror.

———

In times of uncertainty, wait. Always, if you have any doubt, wait. Do not force yourself to any action. If you have a restraint in your spirit, wait until all is clear, and do not go against it.

Mrs. Charles E. Cowman

The great freedom Jesus gives us is to be ourselves, defined by His love and our inner qualities and gifts rather than by any kind of show we put on for the world.

Leslie Williams

THE LOVE OF MONEY

For the love of money is a root of all sorts of evil, and some by longing for it have wandered away from the faith and pierced themselves with many griefs.

1 Timothy 6:10 NASB

Our society is in love with money and the things that money can buy. God is not. God cares about people, not possessions, and so must we. We must, to the best of our abilities, love our neighbors as ourselves, and we must, to the best of our abilities, resist the mighty temptation to place possessions ahead of people.

Money, in and of itself, is not evil; worshipping money is. So today, as you prioritize matters of importance for you and yours, remember that God is almighty, but the dollar is not. If we worship God, we are blessed. But if we worship "the almighty dollar," we are inevitably punished because of our misplaced priorities—and our punishment inevitably comes sooner rather than later.

Have you prayed about your resources lately? Find out how God wants you to use your time and your money. No matter what it costs, forsake all that is not of God.

Kay Arthur

GLORIOUS OPPORTUNITIES

Make the most of every opportunity.

Colossians 4:5 NIV

Are you excited about the opportunities of today and thrilled by the possibilities of tomorrow? Do you confidently expect God to lead you to a place of abundance, peace, and joy? And, when your days on earth are over, do you expect to receive the priceless gift of eternal life? If you trust God's promises, and if you have welcomed God's Son into your heart, then you believe that your future is intensely and eternally bright.

Today, as you prepare to meet the duties of everyday life, pause and consider God's promises. And then think for a moment about the wonderful future that awaits all believers, including you. God has promised that your future is secure. Trust that promise, and celebrate the life of abundance and eternal joy that is now yours through Christ.

Worry is the senseless process of cluttering up tomorrow's opportunities with leftover problems from today.

Barbara Johnson

He who waits until circumstances completely favor his undertaking will never accomplish anything.

Martin Luther

THE POWER
OF PERSEVERANCE

I do not consider myself yet to have taken hold of it. But one thing I do: Forgetting what is behind and straining toward what is ahead, I press on toward the goal to win the prize for which God has called me heavenward in Christ Jesus.

Philippians 3:13-14 NIV

A well-lived life calls for preparation, determination, and, of course, lots of perseverance. As an example of perfect perseverance, we Christians need look no further than our Savior, Jesus Christ. Jesus finished what He began. Despite His suffering, despite the shame of the cross, Jesus was steadfast in His faithfulness to God. We, too, must remain faithful, especially during times of hardship. Sometimes, God may answer our prayers with silence, and when He does, we must patiently persevere.

Are you facing a tough situation? If so, remember this: whatever your problem, God can handle it. Your job is to keep persevering until He does.

Your life is not a boring stretch of highway. It's a straight line to heaven. And just look at the fields ripening along the way. Look at the tenacity and endurance. Look at the grains of righteousness. You'll have quite a crop at harvest . . . so don't give up!

Joni Eareckson Tada

FIRST THINGS FIRST

And I pray this: that your love will keep on growing in knowledge and every kind of discernment, so that you can determine what really matters and can be pure and blameless in the day of Christ.

Philippians 1:9 HCSB

"First things first." These words are easy to speak but hard to put into practice. For busy women living in a demanding world, placing first things first can be difficult indeed. Why? Because so many people are expecting so many things from us!

If you're having trouble prioritizing your day, perhaps you've been trying to organize your life according to your own plans, not God's. A better strategy, of course, is to take your daily obligations and place them in the hands of the One who created you. To do so, you must prioritize your day according to God's commandments, and you must seek His will and His wisdom in all matters. Then, you can face the day with the assurance that the same God who created our universe out of nothingness will help you place first things first in your own life. So, turn the concerns of this day over to God—prayerfully, earnestly, and often. Then listen for His answer . . . and trust the answer He gives.

It may take a lifetime to learn to focus on God, to pull our gaze off the world, off ourselves, off our goals, and to fully gaze on him and worship him.

Mary Morrison Suggs

BEING GENTLE
WITH YOURSELF

You're blessed when you're content with just who you are—no more, no less. That's the moment you find yourselves proud owners of everything that can't be bought.

Matthew 5:5 MSG

Being patient with other people can be difficult. But sometimes, we find it even more difficult to be patient with ourselves. We have high expectations and lofty goals. We want to receive God's blessings now, not later. And, of course, we want our lives to unfold according to our own wishes and our own timetables—not God's. Yet throughout the Bible, we are instructed that patience is the companion of wisdom. Proverbs 16:32 teaches us that "Patience is better than strength" (NCV). God's message, then, is clear: we must be patient with all people, beginning with that particular woman who stares back at us each time we gaze into the mirror.

The Bible affirms the importance of self-acceptance by exhorting believers to love others as they love themselves (Matthew 22:37-40). Furthermore, the Bible teaches that when we genuinely open our hearts to Him, God accepts us just as we are. And, if He accepts us—faults and all—then who are we to believe otherwise?

SERENITY

The Lord says, "Forget what happened before, and do not think about the past. Look at the new thing I am going to do. It is already happening. Don't you see it? I will make a road in the desert and rivers in the dry land."

Isaiah 43:18-19 NCV

The American theologian Reinhold Niebuhr composed a profoundly simple verse that came to be known as the Serenity Prayer: "God, grant me the serenity to accept the things I cannot change, the courage to change the things I can, and the wisdom to know the difference." Niebuhr's words are far easier to recite than they are to live by. Why? Because most of us want life to unfold in accordance with our own wishes and timetables. But sometimes God has other plans.

If you've encountered unfortunate circumstances that are beyond your power to control, accept those circumstances . . . and trust God. When you do, you can be comforted in the knowledge that your Creator is both loving and wise, and that He understands His plans perfectly, even when you do not.

Loving Him means the thankful acceptance of all things that His love has appointed.

Elisabeth Elliot

CONQUERING OUR FRUSTRATIONS

People with quick tempers cause trouble, but those who control their tempers stop a quarrel.

Proverbs 15:18 NCV

Life is full of frustrations: some great and some small. On occasion, you, like Jesus, will confront evil, and when you do, you may respond as He did: vigorously and without reservation. But, more often your frustrations will be of the more mundane variety. As long as you live here on earth, you will face countless opportunities to lose your temper over small, relatively insignificant events: a traffic jam, a spilled cup of coffee, an inconsiderate comment, a broken promise.

When you are tempted to lose your temper over the minor inconveniences of life, don't. Turn away from anger, hatred, bitterness, and regret. Turn instead to God. When you do, you'll be following His commandments and giving yourself a priceless gift . . . the gift of peace.

Life is too short to spend it being angry, bored, or dull.

Barbara Johnson

IN HIS IMAGE

So God created man in his own image, in the image of God he created him; male and female he created them.

Genesis 1:27 NIV

What is your attitude today? Are you fearful or worried? Are you more concerned about pleasing your friends than about pleasing your God? Are you bitter, confused, cynical, or pessimistic? If so, it's time to have a little chat with your Father in heaven.

God intends that your life be filled with spiritual abundance and joy—but God will not force His joy upon you—you must claim it for yourself. So do yourself this favor: accept God's gifts with a smile on your face, a song on your lips, and joy in your heart. Think optimistically about yourself and your future. Give thanks to the One who has given you everything, and trust in your heart that He wants to give you so much more.

The Reference Point for the Christian is the Bible. All values, judgments, and attitudes must be gauged in relationship to this Reference Point.

Ruth Bell Graham

God has given you special talents—now it's your turn to give them back to God.

Marie T. Freeman

THE GUIDEBOOK

There's nothing like the written Word of God for showing you the way to salvation through faith in Christ Jesus. Every part of Scripture is God-breathed and useful one way or another, showing us truth, exposing our rebellion, correcting our mistakes, training us to live God's way. Through the Word we are put together and shaped up for the tasks God has for us.

2 Timothy 3:15-17 MSG

God has given us a guidebook for righteous living called the Holy Bible. It contains thorough instructions which, if followed, lead to fulfillment, righteousness, and salvation. But, if we choose to ignore God's commandments, the results are as predictable as they are tragic.

God has given us the Bible for the purpose of knowing His promises, His power, His commandments, His wisdom, His love, and His Son. As we study God's teachings and apply them to our lives, we live by the Word that shall never pass away. Today, let us follow God's commandments, and let us conduct our lives in such a way that we might be shining examples to our families, and, most importantly, to those who have not yet found Christ.

Unless we form the habit of going to the Bible in bright moments as well as in trouble, we cannot fully respond to its consolations because we lack equilibrium between light and darkness.

Helen Keller

A HELPING HAND

Then a Samaritan traveling down the road came to where the hurt man was. When he saw the man, he felt very sorry for him. The Samaritan went to him, poured olive oil and wine on his wounds, and bandaged them. Then he put the hurt man on his own donkey and took him to an inn where he cared for him.

Luke 10:33-34 NCV

Sometimes we would like to help make the world a better place, but we're not sure how to do it. Jesus told the story of the "Good Samaritan," a man who helped a fellow traveler when no one else would. We, too, should be good Samaritans when we find people who need our help.

When bad things happen in our world, there's always something we can do. So what can you do to make God's world a better place? You can start by making your own corner of the world a little nicer place to live (by sharing kind words and good deeds). And then, you can take your concerns to God in prayer. Whether you've offered a helping hand or a heartfelt prayer, you've done a lot.

I never look at the masses as my responsibility. I look at the individual. I can love only one person at a time. I can feed only one person at a time. Just one, one, one. You get closer to Christ by coming closer to each other.

Mother Teresa

CHOICES, CHOICES, CHOICES

Cheerfully pleasing God is the main thing, and that's what we aim to do, regardless of our conditions.

2 Corinthians 5:9 MSG

Your life is a series of choices. From the instant you wake up in the morning until the moment you nod off to sleep at night, you make lots of decisions: decisions about the things you do, decisions about the words you speak, and decisions about the thoughts you choose to think. Simply put, the quality of those decisions determines the quality of your life.

So, if you sincerely want to lead a life that is pleasing to God, you must make choices that are pleasing to Him. He deserves no less . . . and neither, for that matter, do you.

No matter how many books you read, no matter how many schools you attend, you're never really wise until you start making wise choices.

Marie T. Freeman

God is voting for us all the time. The devil is voting against us all the time. The way we vote carries the election.

Corrie ten Boom

OBEDIENCE NOW

By this we know that we have come to know Him, if we keep His commandments.

1 John 2:3 NASB

In order to enjoy a deeper relationship with God, you must strive diligently to live in accordance with His commandments. But there's a problem—you live in a world that seeks to snare your attention and lead you away from God.

Because you are an imperfect mortal being, you cannot be perfectly obedient, nor does God expect you to be. What is required, however, is a sincere desire to be obedient coupled with an awareness of sin and a willingness to distance yourself from it as soon as you encounter it.

Are you willing to conform your behavior to God's rules? Hopefully, you can answer that question with a resounding yes. Otherwise, you'll never experience a full measure of the blessings that the Creator gives to those who obey Him.

Every century the Church makes a fresh attempt to make Christianity acceptable. But an acceptable Christianity is not Christian; a comprehensible God is no more than an idol.

Madeleine L'Engle

FEEDING THE CHURCH

The church, you see, is not peripheral to the world; the world is peripheral to the church. The church is Christ's body, in which he speaks and acts, by which he fills everything with his presence.

Ephesians 1:23 MSG

One way that we come to know God is by involving ourselves in His church.

In the Book of Acts, Luke reminds us to "feed the church of God" (20:28). As Christians who have been saved by a loving, compassionate Creator, we are compelled not only to worship Him in our hearts but also to worship Him in the presence of fellow believers.

Do you feed the church of God? Do you attend regularly, and are you an active participant? The answer to these questions will have a profound impact on the quality and direction of your spiritual journey.

So do yourself a favor: become actively involved in your church. Don't just go to church out of habit. Go to church out of a sincere desire to know and worship God. When you do, you'll be blessed by the One who sent His Son to die so that you might have everlasting life.

Man was created by God to know and love Him in a permanent, personal relationship.

Anne Graham Lotz

OLD YOU, NEW YOU

If anyone belongs to Christ, there is a new creation. The old things have gone; everything is made new!

2 Corinthians 5:17 NCV

Think, for a moment, about the "old" you, the person you were before you invited Christ to reign over your heart. Now, think about the "new" you, the person you have become since then. Is there a difference between the "old" you and the "new and improved" version? There should be! And that difference should be noticeable not only to you but also to others.

The Bible clearly teaches that when we welcome Christ into our hearts, we become new creations through Him. Our challenge, of course, is to behave ourselves like new creations. When we do, God fills our hearts, He blesses our endeavors, and transforms our lives . . . forever.

The whole idea of belonging to Christ is to look less and less like we used to and more and more like Him.

Angela Thomas

The amazing thing about Jesus is that He doesn't just patch up our lives; He gives us a brand new sheet, a clean slate to start over, all new.

Gloria Gaither

LIFE'S MOUNTAINTOPS, LIFE'S VALLEYS

I sought the LORD, and he answered me; he delivered me from all my fears.

Psalm 34:4 NIV

Every life (including yours) is an unfolding series of events: some fabulous, some not-so-fabulous, and some downright disheartening. When you reach the mountaintops of life, praising God is easy. But, when the storm clouds form overhead, your faith will be tested, sometimes to the breaking point. As a believer, you can take comfort in this fact: Wherever you find yourself, whether at the top of the mountain or the depths of the valley, God is there, and because He cares for you, you can live courageously.

The next time you find your courage tested to the limit, remember that God is your shield and your strength; He is your protector and your deliverer. Call upon Him in your hour of need and He will protect you.

———

Just as courage is faith in good, so discouragement is faith in evil, and, while courage opens the door to good, discouragement opens it to evil.

Hannah Whitall Smith

EXPECTING THE BEST

This is the day the LORD has made; let us rejoice and be glad in it.

Psalm 118:24 NIV

What do you expect from the day ahead? Are you expecting God to do wonderful things, or are you living beneath a cloud of apprehension and doubt? The familiar words of Psalm 118:24 remind us of a profound yet simple truth: "This is the day which the LORD hath made; we will rejoice and be glad in it" (KJV). For believers, every day begins and ends with God's Son and God's promises. When we accept Christ into our hearts, God promises us the opportunity for earthly peace and spiritual abundance. But more importantly, God promises us the priceless gift of eternal life.

As we face the inevitable challenges of life-here-on-earth, we must arm ourselves with the promises of God's Holy Word. When we do, we can expect the best, not only for the day ahead, but also for all eternity.

Make the least of all that goes and the most of all that comes. Don't regret what is past. Cherish what you have. Look forward to all that is to come. And most important of all, rely moment by moment on Jesus Christ.

Gigi Graham Tchividjian

THE REMEDY FOR UNCERTAINTY

He replied, "You of little faith, why are you so afraid?"
Then he got up and rebuked the winds and the waves, and
it was completely calm.

Matthew 8:26 NIV

Sometimes, like Jesus' disciples, we feel threatened by the storms of life. During these moments, when our hearts are flooded with uncertainty, we must remember that God is not simply near, He is here.

Have you ever felt your faith in God slipping away? If so, you are in good company. Even the most faithful Christians are, at times, beset by occasional bouts of discouragement and doubt. But even when you feel far removed from God, God never leaves your side. He is always with you, always willing to calm the storms of life. When you sincerely seek His presence—and when you genuinely seek to establish a deeper, more meaningful relationship with His Son—God will calm your fears, answer your prayers, and restore your soul.

I was learning something important: we are most vulnerable to the piercing winds of doubt when we distance ourselves from the mission and fellowship to which Christ has called us. Our night of discouragement will seem endless and our task impossible, unless we recognize that He stands in our midst.

Joni Eareckson Tada

THANKSGIVING YES . . .
ENVY NO!

Stop your anger! Turn from your rage! Do not envy others—it only leads to harm.

Psalm 37:8 NLT

As the recipient of God's grace, you have every reason to celebrate life. After all, God has promised you the opportunity to receive His abundance and His joy—in fact, you have the opportunity to receive those gifts right now. But if you allow envy to gnaw away at the fabric of your soul, you'll find that joy remains elusive. So do yourself an enormous favor: Rather than succumbing to the sin of envy, focus on the marvelous things that God has done for you—starting with Christ's sacrifice. Thank the Giver of all good gifts, and keep thanking Him for the wonders of His love and the miracles of His creation. Count your own blessings and let your neighbors count theirs. It's the godly way to live.

Discontent dries up the soul.

Elisabeth Elliot

A PRAYER

Dear Lord, deliver me from the needless pain of envy. You have given me countless blessings. Let me be thankful for the gifts I have received, and let me never be resentful of the gifts You have given others. Amen

COMPETENCE, NOT EXCUSES

Do you see people skilled in their work? They will work for kings, not for ordinary people.

Proverbs 22:29 NCV

Excuses are everywhere . . . excellence is not. If you seek excellence (and the rewards that accompany it), you must avoid the bad habit of making excuses.

Whatever your job description, it's up to you, and no one else, to become a master of your craft. It's up to you to do your job right—and to do it right now. When you do, you'll discover that excellence is its own reward . . . but not its only reward.

We need to stop focusing on our lacks and stop giving out excuses and start looking at and listening to Jesus.

Anne Graham Lotz

A PRAYER

Dear Lord, I will strive to become a woman of dedication and skill. Today, I will do my best, and I will expect the best. Amen

GOD'S PLAN FOR
YOUR FAMILY

Unless the Lord builds a house, its builders labor over it in vain; unless the Lord watches over a city, the watchman stays alert in vain.

Psalm 127:1 HCSB

As you consider God's purpose for your own life, you must also consider how your plans will effect the most important people that God has entrusted to your care: your loved ones.

A loving family is a treasure from God. If you happen to be a member of a close knit, supportive clan, offer a word of thanks to your Creator. He has blessed you with one of His most precious earthly possessions. Your obligation, in response to God's gift, is to treat your family in ways that are consistent with His commandments. So, as you prayerfully seek God's direction, remember that He has important plans for your home life as well as your professional life. It's up to you to act—and to plan—accordingly.

It is easy to love the people far way. It is not always easy to love those close to us. It is easier to give a cup of rice to relieve hunger than to relieve the loneliness and pain of someone unloved in our own home. Bring love into your home, for this is where our love for each other must start.

Mother Teresa

OUR FEAR-BASED WORLD

They won't be afraid of bad news; their hearts are steady because they trust the Lord.

Psalm 112:7 NCV

We live in a fear-based world, a world where bad news travels at light speed and good news doesn't. These are troubled times, times when we have legitimate fears for the future of our nation, our world, and our families. But as Christians, we have every reason to live courageously. After all, the ultimate battle has already been fought and won on that faraway cross at Calvary.

Perhaps you, like countless other believers, have found your courage tested by the anxieties and fears that are an inevitable part of 21st-century life. If so, God wants to have a little chat with you. The next time you find your courage tested to the limit, God wants to remind you that He is not just near, He is here. So remember this: your Heavenly Father is your Protector and your Deliverer. Call upon Him in your hour of need, and be comforted. Whatever your challenge, whatever your trouble, God can handle it. And will.

His hand on me is a father's hand, gently guiding and encouraging. His hand lets me know he is with me, so I am not afraid.

Mary Morrison Suggs

A WILLINGNESS TO FORGIVE

Be kind to one another, tender-hearted, forgiving each other, just as God in Christ also has forgiven you.

Ephesians 4:32 NASB

To forgive others is difficult. Being frail, fallible, imperfect human beings, we are quick to anger, quick to blame, slow to forgive, and even slower to forget. No matter. Forgiveness, no matter how difficult, is God's way, and it must be our way, too.

God's commandments are not intended to be customized for the particular whims of particular believers. God's Word is not a menu from which each of us may select items à la carte, according to our own desires. Far from it. God's Holy Word is a book that must be taken in its entirety; all of God's commandments are to be taken seriously. And, so it is with forgiveness. So, if you hold bitterness against even a single person, forgive. Then, to the best of your abilities, forget. It's God's way for you to live.

———

There is nothing, absolutely nothing, that God will not forgive. You cannot "out-sin" His forgiveness. You cannot "out-sin" the love of God.

Kathy Troccoli

Our relationships with other people are of primary importance to God. Because God is love, He cannot tolerate any unforgiveness or hardness in us toward any individual.

Catherine Marshall

OFFERING THANKS

In everything give thanks; for this is the will of God in Christ Jesus for you.

1 Thessalonians 5:18 NKJV

Sometimes, life can be complicated, demanding, and frustrating. When the demands of life leave us rushing from place to place with scarcely a moment to spare, we may fail to pause and thank our Creator for His gifts. But, whenever we neglect to give proper thanks to the Father, we suffer because of our misplaced priorities.

Today, begin making a list of your blessings. You most certainly will not be able to make a complete list, but take a few moments and jot down as many blessings as you can. Then, give thanks to the Giver of all good things: God. His love for you is eternal, as are His gifts. And it's never too soon—or too late—to offer Him thanks.

God's love for His children is unconditional, no strings attached. But, God's blessings on our lives do come with a condition—obedience. If we are to receive the fullness of God's blessings, we must obey Him and keep His commandments.

Mary Prince

No duty is more urgent than that of returning thanks.

St. Ambrose

HIS AWESOME CREATION

And to every beast of the earth and to every bird of the sky and to every thing that moves on the earth which has life . . . God saw all that He had made, and behold, it was very good.

Genesis 1:30-31 NASB

When we consider God's glorious universe, we marvel at the miracle of nature. The smallest seedlings and grandest stars are all part of God's infinite creation. God has placed His handiwork on display for all to see, and if we are wise, we will make time each day to celebrate the world that surrounds us.

Today, as you fulfill the demands of everyday life, pause to consider the majesty of heaven and earth. It is as miraculous as it is beautiful, as incomprehensible as it is breathtaking.

The Psalmist reminds us that the heavens are a declaration of God's glory (Psalm 19:1). May we never cease to praise the Father for a universe that stands as an awesome testimony to His presence and His power.

How awesome that the "Word" that was in the beginning, by which and through which God created everything, was—and is—a living Person with a mind, will, emotions, and intellect.

Anne Graham Lotz

HIS INTIMATE LOVE

As the Father loved Me, I also have loved you; abide in My love.

John 15:9 NKJV

St. Augustine observed, "God loves each of us as if there were only one of us." Do you believe those words? Do you seek an intimate, one-on-one relationship with your Heavenly Father, or are you satisfied to keep Him at a "safe" distance?

Sometimes, in the crush of our daily duties, God may seem far away, but He is not. God is everywhere we have ever been and everywhere we will ever go. He is with us night and day; He knows our thoughts and our prayers. And, when we earnestly seek Him, we will find Him because He is here, waiting patiently for us to reach out to Him. May we reach out to Him today and always. And may we praise Him for the glorious gifts that have transformed us today and forever.

Our hearts have been made to cry out for a love that can come only from our Creator.

Angela Thomas

The love of God is so vast, the power of his touch so invigorating, we could just stay in his presence for hours, soaking up his glory, basking in His blessings.

Debra Evans

HE REIGNS

In all your ways acknowledge Him, and He shall direct your paths.

Proverbs 3:6 NKJV

God is sovereign. He reigns over the entire universe and He reigns over your little corner of that universe. Your challenge is to recognize God's sovereignty and live in accordance with His commandments. Sometimes, of course, this is easier said than done.

Your Heavenly Father may not always reveal Himself as quickly (or as clearly) as you would like. But rest assured: God is in control, God is here, and God intends to use you in wonderful, unexpected ways. He desires to lead you along a path of His choosing. Your challenge is to watch, to listen, to learn . . . and to follow.

As you place yourself under the sovereign lordship of Jesus Christ, each mistake or failure can lead you right back to the throne.

Barbara Johnson

With each new experience of letting God be in control, we gain courage and reinforcement for daring to do it again and again.

Gloria Gaither

IS THE GOLDEN RULE
YOUR RULE?

*And let us not grow weary while doing good, for in due
season we shall reap if we do not lose heart.*

Galatians 6:9 NKJV

Would you like to make the world a better place
and feel better about yourself at the same time? If so,
you can start by practicing the Golden Rule.

The Bible teaches us to treat other people with
respect, kindness, courtesy, and love. When we do,
we make other people happy, we make God happy,
and we feel better about ourselves.

So if you're wondering how to make the world—
and your world—a better place, here's a great place
to start: let the Golden Rule be your rule. And if
you want to know how to treat other people, ask the
woman you see every time you glance in the mirror.

Sometimes one little spark of kindness is all it takes
to reignite the light of hope in a heart that's blinded
by pain.

Barbara Johnson

We should behave to our friends as we would wish
our friends to behave to us.

Aristotle

HEALTHY CHOICES

I shall yet praise him, who is the health of my countenance, and my God.

Psalm 42:11 KJV

The journey toward improved health is not only a common-sense exercise in personal discipline; it is also a spiritual journey ordained by our Creator. God does not intend that we abuse our bodies by giving in to excessive appetites or to slothful behavior. To the contrary, God has instructed us to protect our physical bodies to the greatest extent we can. To do otherwise is to disobey Him.

God's plan for you includes provisions for your spiritual, physical, and emotional health. But, He expects you to do your fair share of the work! In a world that is chock-full of tasty temptations, you may find it all too easy to make unhealthy choices. Your challenge, of course, is to resist those unhealthy temptations by every means you can, including prayer. And rest assured: when you ask for God's help, He will give it.

Our body is like armor, our soul like the warrior. Take care of both, and you will be ready for what comes.

Amma St. Syncletice

THE SELF-FULFILLING PROPHECY

May He grant you according to your heart's desire, and fulfill all your purpose.

Psalm 20:4 NKJV

The self-fulfilling prophecy is alive, well, and living at your house. If you trust God and have faith for the future, your optimistic beliefs will give you direction and motivation. That's one reason that you should never lose hope, but certainly not the only reason. The primary reason that you, as a believer, should never lose hope, is because of God's unfailing promises.

Make no mistake about it: thoughts are powerful things: your thoughts have the power to lift you up or to hold you down. When you acquire the habit of hopeful thinking, you will have acquired a powerful tool for improving your life. So if you fall into the habit of negative thinking, think again. After all, God's Word teaches us that Christ can overcome every difficulty (John 16:33). And when God makes a promise, He keeps it.

The most profane word we use is "hopeless." When you say a situation or person is hopeless, you are slamming the door in the face of God.

Kathy Troccoli

THE VOICE OF GOD

Listen in silence before me . . . .

Isaiah 41:1 NLT

Sometimes God speaks loudly and clearly. More often, He speaks in a quiet voice—and if you are wise, you will be listening carefully when He does. To do so, you must carve out quiet moments each day to study His Word and sense His direction.

Can you quiet yourself long enough to listen to your conscience? Are you attuned to the subtle guidance of your intuition? Are you willing to pray sincerely and then to wait quietly for God's response. Hopefully so. Usually God refrains from sending His messages on stone tablets or city billboards. More often, He communicates in subtler ways. If you sincerely desire to hear His voice, you must listen carefully, and you must do so in the silent corners of your quiet, willing heart.

When we come to Jesus stripped of pretensions, with a needy spirit, ready to listen, He meets us at the point of need.

Catherine Marshall

When I am constantly running there is no time for being. When there is no time for being there is no time for listening.

Madeleine L'Engle

YOUR SPIRITUAL JOURNEY

*Know the love of Christ which surpasses knowledge, that
you may be filled up to all the fullness of God.*

Ephesians 3:19 NASB

The journey toward spiritual maturity lasts a
lifetime. As Christians, we can and should continue
to grow in the love and the knowledge of our Savior
as long as we live. When we cease to grow, either
emotionally or spiritually, we do ourselves a profound
disservice. But, if we study God's Word, if we obey
His commandments, and if we live in the center of
His will, we will not be "stagnant" believers; we will,
instead, be healthy, growing Christians.

Life is a series of decisions. Each day, we make
countless decisions that can bring us closer to God
. . . or not. When we live according to the principles
contained in God's Holy Word, we embark upon
a journey of spiritual maturity that results in life
abundant and life eternal.

One of the marks of Spiritual maturity is a consistent,
Spirit-controlled life.

Vonette Bright

A PRAYER

Thank You, Lord, that I am not yet what I am to
become. The Holy Scripture tells me that You are at
work in my life, continuing to help me grow and to
mature in the faith. Show me Your wisdom, Father,
and let me live according to Your Word and Your
will. Amen

MAKING PEACE
WITH YOUR PAST

The Lord says, "Forget what happened before, and do not think about the past. Look at the new thing I am going to do. It is already happening. Don't you see it? I will make a road in the desert and rivers in the dry land."

Isaiah 43:18-19 NCV

Have you made peace with your past? If so, congratulations. But, if you are mired in the quicksand of regret, it's time to plan your escape. How can you do so? By accepting what has been and by trusting God for what will be.

Because you are human, you may be slow to forget yesterday's disappointments. But, if you sincerely seek to focus your hopes and energies on the future, then you must find ways to accept the past, no matter how difficult it may be to do so. So, if you have not yet made peace with the past, today is the day to declare an end to all hostilities. When you do, you can then turn your thoughts to wondrous promises of God and to the glorious future that He has in store for you.

We can't just put our pasts behind us. We've got to put our pasts in front of God.

Beth Moore

THE CHAINS OF PERFECTIONISM

Those who wait for perfect weather will never plant seeds;
those who look at every cloud will never harvest crops.

Ecclesiastes 11:4 NCV

The media delivers an endless stream of messages that tell you how to look, how to behave, and how to dress. The media's expectations are impossible to meet—God's are not. God doesn't expect perfection . . . and neither should you.

If you find yourself bound up by the chains of perfectionism, it's time to ask yourself who you're trying to impress, and why. If you're trying to impress other people, it's time to reconsider your priorities. Your first responsibility is to the Heavenly Father who created you and to His Son who saved you. Then, you bear a powerful responsibility to your family. But, when it comes to meeting society's unrealistic expectations, forget it! After all, pleasing God is simply a matter of obeying His commandments and accepting His Son. But as for pleasing everybody else? That's impossible!

Excellence is not perfection, but essentially a desire to be strong in the Lord and for the Lord.

Cynthia Heald

SOLVING PROBLEMS

People who do what is right may have many problems, but the Lord will solve them all.

Psalm 34:19 NCV

Life is an exercise in problem-solving. The question is not whether we will encounter problems; the real question is how we will choose to address them. When it comes to solving the problems of everyday living, we often know precisely what needs to be done, but we may be slow in doing it—especially if what needs to be done is difficult or uncomfortable for us. So we put off till tomorrow what should be done today.

The words of Psalm 34 remind us that the Lord solves problems for "people who do what is right." And usually, doing "what is right" means doing the uncomfortable work of confronting our problems sooner rather than later. So with no further ado, let the problem-solving begin . . . now.

What a comfort to know that God is present there in your life, available to meet every situation with you, that you are never left to face any problem alone.

Vonette Bright

Never use your problem as an excuse for bad attitudes or behavior.

Joyce Meyer

THE SIMPLE LIFE

Whoever becomes simple and elemental again, like this child, will rank high in God's kingdom.

Matthew 18:4 MSG

You live in a world where simplicity is in short supply. Think for a moment about the complexity of your everyday life and compare it to the lives of your ancestors. Certainly, you are the beneficiary of many technological innovations, but those innovations have a price: in all likelihood, your world is highly complex.

Unless you take firm control of your time and your life, you may be overwhelmed by an ever-increasing tidal wave of complexity that threatens your happiness. But your Heavenly Father understands the joy of living simply, and so should you. So do yourself a favor: keep your life as simple as possible. Simplicity is, indeed, genius. By simplifying your life, you are destined to improve it.

Nobody is going to simplify your life for you. You've got to simplify things for yourself.

Marie T. Freeman

I am beginning to learn that it is the sweet, simple things of life which are the real ones after all.

Laura Ingalls Wilder

SHOUT FOR JOY

Shout for joy to the LORD, all the earth. Worship the LORD with gladness; come before him with joyful songs.

Psalm 100:1-2 NIV

The 100th Psalm reminds us that the entire earth should "Shout for joy to the Lord." As God's children, we are blessed beyond measure, but sometimes, as busy women living in a demanding world, we are slow to count our gifts and even slower to give thanks to the Giver.

Our blessings include life and health, family and friends, freedom and possessions—for starters. And, the gifts we receive from God are multiplied when we share them. May we always give thanks to God for His blessings, and may we always demonstrate our gratitude by sharing our gifts with others. The 118th Psalm reminds us that, "This is the day which the LORD has made; let us rejoice and be glad in it" (v. 24, NASB). May we celebrate this day and the One who created it.

If you can forgive the person you were, accept the person you are, and believe in the person you will become, you are headed for joy. So celebrate your life.

Barbara Johnson

TURNING AWAY FROM ANGER

*My dear brothers and sisters, always be willing to listen
and slow to speak. Do not become angry easily, because
anger will not help you live the right kind of life God
wants.*

James 1:19-20 NCV

Perhaps God gave each of us one mouth and two
ears in order that we might listen twice as much as
we speak. Unfortunately, many of us do otherwise,
especially when we become angry.

Anger is a natural human emotion that is
sometimes necessary and appropriate. Even Jesus
Himself became angered when He confronted the
moneychangers in the temple. But, more often than
not, our frustrations are of the more mundane variety.
When you are tempted to lose your temper over the
minor inconveniences of life, don't. Turn away from
anger, and turn instead to God.

When the winds are cold, and the days are long, and
thy soul from care would hide, fly back, fly back, to
thy Father then, and beneath His wings abide.

Fanny Crosby

Why lose your temper if, by doing so, you offend God,
annoy other people, give yourself a bad time . . . and,
in the end, have to find it again?

Josemaria Escriva

COUNTING YOUR BLESSINGS

And now, dear brothers and sisters, let me say one more thing as I close this letter. Fix your thoughts on what is true and honorable and right. Think about things that are pure and lovely and admirable. Think about things that are excellent and worthy of praise.

Philippians 4:8 NLT

How will you direct your thoughts today? Will you obey the words of Philippians 4:8 by dwelling upon those things that are true and honorable and right? Or will you allow your thoughts to be hijacked by the negativity that seems to dominate our troubled world? Are you fearful, angry, bored, or worried? Are you so preoccupied with the concerns of this day that you fail to thank God for the promise of eternity? Are you confused, bitter, or pessimistic? If so, God wants to have a little talk with you.

God intends that you experience joy and abundance. So, today and every day hereafter, celebrate the life that God has given you by focusing your thoughts upon those things that are worthy of praise. Today, count your blessings instead of your hardships. And thank the Giver of all things good for gifts that are simply too numerous to count.

The greater part of our happiness or misery depends on our dispositions, and not on our circumstances.

Martha Washington

NOURISHED BY THE WORD

You will be a good servant of Christ Jesus, constantly nourished on the words of the faith and of the sound doctrine which you have been following.

1 Timothy 4:6 NASB

Do you read your Bible a lot . . . or not? The answer to this simple question will determine, to a surprising extent, the quality of your life and the direction of your faith.

As you establish priorities for life, you must decide whether God's Word will be a bright spotlight that guides your path every day or a tiny nightlight that occasionally flickers in the dark. The decision to study the Bible—or not—is yours and yours alone. But make no mistake: how you choose to use your Bible will have a profound impact on you and your loved ones.

The Bible is the ultimate guide for life; make it your guidebook as well. When you do, you can be comforted in the knowledge that your steps are guided by a Source of wisdom and truth that never fails.

If we neglect the Bible, we cannot expect to benefit from the wisdom and direction that result from knowing God's Word.

Vonette Bright

TOO BUSY

Careful planning puts you ahead in the long run; hurry and scurry puts you further behind.

Proverbs 21:5 MSG

Are you one of those women who is simply too busy for your own good? Has the hectic pace of life robbed you of the peace that might otherwise be yours through Jesus Christ? If so, you're doing a disservice to yourself and your family.

Through His Son Jesus, God offers you a peace that passes human understanding, but He won't force His peace upon you; in order to experience it, you must slow down long enough to sense His presence and His love.

Today, as a gift to yourself, to your family, and to the world, be still and claim the inner peace that is your spiritual birthright—the peace of Jesus Christ. It is offered freely; it has been paid for in full; it is yours for the asking. So ask. And then share.

How much of our lives are, well, so daily. How often our hours are filled with the mundane, seemingly unimportant things that have to be done, whether at home or work. These very "daily" tasks could become a celebration of praise. "It is through consecration," someone has said, "that drudgery is made divine."

Gigi Graham Tchividjian

THE GIFT OF CHEERFULNESS

Worry is a heavy load, but a kind word cheers you up.

Proverbs 12:25 NCV

Cheerfulness is a gift that we give to others and to ourselves. And, as believers who have been saved by a risen Christ, why shouldn't we be cheerful? The answer, of course, is that we have every reason to honor our Savior with joy in our hearts, smiles on our faces, and words of celebration on our lips.

Christ promises us lives of abundance and joy if we accept His love and His grace. Yet sometimes, even the most righteous among us are beset by fits of ill temper and frustration. During these moments, we may not feel like turning our thoughts and prayers to Christ, but that's precisely what we should do. When we do so, we simply can't stay grumpy for long.

The greatest honor you can give Almighty God is to live gladly and joyfully because of the knowledge of His love.

Juliana of Norwich

A PRAYER

Dear Lord, You have given me so many reasons to celebrate. Today, let me choose an attitude of cheerfulness. Let me be a joyful Christian, Lord, quick to smile and slow to anger. And, let me share Your goodness with all whom I meet so that Your love might shine in me and through me. Amen

A GROWING RELATIONSHIP WITH GOD

But grow in the grace and knowledge of our Lord and Savior Jesus Christ.

2 Peter 3:18 NIV

Your relationship with God is ongoing; it unfolds day by day, and it offers countless opportunities to grow closer to Him . . . or not. As each new day unfolds, you are confronted with a wide range of decisions: how you will behave, where you will direct your thoughts, with whom you will associate, and what you will choose to worship. These choices, along with many others like them, are yours and yours alone. How you choose determines how your relationship with God will unfold.

Are you continuing to grow in your love and knowledge of the Lord, or are you "satisfied" with the current state of your spiritual health? Hopefully, you're determined to make yourself a growing Christian. Your Savior deserves no less, and neither, by the way, do you.

The things God delights in, kindness, justice, and righteousness, are the essence of Christianity. If he delights in these things, then his followers must also.

Mary Morrison Suggs

LOVE AND COMMITMENT

If you falter in times of trouble, how small is your strength!

Proverbs 24:10 NIV

In God's program, the words "love" and "commitment" are intertwined. According to God, genuine love is patient, unselfish, and kind, but it goes beyond that—genuine love is committed love, and that means that genuine love is more than a feeling . . . it is a decision to make love endure, no matter what.

Unfortunately, we live in a world where marriage vows are taken far too lightly. Too many couples are far too quick to push the panic button—or the eject button.

If you're a married woman who has vowed to love your partner "till death do you part," then you must take that vow very seriously. And one more thing: you'd better put God right where He belongs: at the absolute center of your marriage.

So I go to church, not because of any legalistic or moralistic reasons, but because I am a hungry sheep who needs to be fed; and for the same reason that I wear a wedding ring: a public witness of a private commitment.

Madeleine L'Engle

THE VOICE INSIDE YOUR HEAD

So I strive always to keep my conscience clear . . . .
Acts 24:16 NIV

When you're about to do something that you know is wrong, a little voice inside your head has a way of speaking up. That voice, of course, is your conscience: an early-warning system designed to keep you out of trouble. If you listen to that voice, you'll be okay; if you ignore it, you're asking for headaches or heartbreaks, or both.

Whenever you're about to make an important decision, you should listen carefully to the quiet voice inside. Sometimes, of course, it's tempting to do otherwise. From time to time you'll be tempted to abandon your better judgement by ignoring your conscience. But remember: a conscience is a terrible thing to waste. So instead of ignoring that quiet little voice, pay careful attention to it. If you do, your conscience will lead you in the right direction—in fact, it's trying to lead you right now. So listen . . . and learn.

A PRAYER

Dear God, You've given me a conscience that tells me right from wrong. Let me trust my conscience, and let me live according to Your teachings, not just for today, but forever. Amen

COURTESY MATTERS

Out of respect for Christ, be courteously reverent to one another.

Ephesians 5:21 MSG

Did Christ instruct us in matters of etiquette and courtesy? Of course He did. Christ's instructions are clear: "In everything, therefore, treat people the same way you want them to treat you, for this is the Law and the Prophets" (Matthew 7:12 NASB). Jesus did not say, "In some things, treat people as you wish to be treated." And, He did not say, "From time to time, treat others with kindness." Christ said that we should treat others as we wish to be treated in every aspect of our daily lives. This, of course, is a tall order indeed, but as Christians, we are commanded to do our best.

Today, be a little kinder than necessary to family members, friends, and total strangers. And, as you consider all the things that Christ has done in your life, honor Him with your words and with your deeds. He expects no less, and He deserves no less.

Courtesy is contagious.

Marie T. Freeman

A PRAYER

Lord, You have created each person in Your own image; let me honor those who cross my path with the dignity that You have bestowed upon them. We are all Your children, Lord; let me show kindness to all. Amen

BEYOND THE DIFFICULTIES

It will be hard when all these things happen to you. But after that you will come back to the Lord your God and obey him, because the Lord your God is a merciful God. He will not leave you or destroy you. He will not forget the Agreement with your ancestors, which he swore to them.

Deuteronomy 4:30-31 NCV

Sometimes the traffic jams, and sometimes the dog gobbles the homework. But, when we find ourselves overtaken by the minor frustrations of life, we must catch ourselves, take a deep breath, and lift our thoughts upward. Although we are here on earth struggling to rise above the distractions of the day, we need never struggle alone. God is here—eternally and faithfully, with infinite patience and love—and, if we reach out to Him, He will restore perspective and peace to our souls.

If you find yourself enduring difficult circumstances, remember that God remains in His heaven. If you become discouraged with the direction of your day or your life, lift your thoughts and prayers to Him. He will guide you through your difficulties and beyond them.

Do the unpleasant work first and enjoy the rest of the day.

Marie T. Freeman

BIG DREAMS

With God's power working in us, God can do much, much more than anything we can ask or imagine.

Ephesians 3:20 NCV

Are you willing to entertain the possibility that God has big plans in store for you? Hopefully so. Yet sometimes, especially if you've recently experienced a life-altering disappointment, you may find it difficult to envision a brighter future for yourself and your family. If so, it's time to reconsider your own capabilities . . . and God's.

Your Heavenly Father created you with unique gifts and untapped talents; your job is to tap them. When you do, you'll begin to feel an increasing sense of confidence in yourself and in your future. So even if you're experiencing difficult days, don't abandon your dreams. Instead, trust that God is preparing you for greater things.

The future lies all before us. Shall it only be a slight advance upon what we usually do? Ought it not to be a bound, a leap forward to altitudes of endeavor and success undreamed of before?

Annie Armstrong

God created us with an overwhelming desire to soar. He designed us to be tremendously productive and "to mount up with wings like eagles," realistically dreaming of what He can do with our potential.

Carol Kent

ENTHUSIASM FOR CHRIST

*So roll up your sleeves, put your mind in gear, be totally
ready to receive the gift that's coming when Jesus arrives.
Don't lazily slip back into those old grooves of evil, doing
just what you feel like doing. You didn't know any better
then; you do now. As obedient children, let yourselves
be pulled into a way of life shaped by God's life, a life
energetic and blazing with holiness.*

1 Peter 1:13-15 MSG

John Wesley advised, "Catch on fire with
enthusiasm and people will come for miles to watch
you burn." His words still ring true. When we fan the
flames of enthusiasm for Christ, our faith serves as a
beacon to others.

Our world desperately needs faithful women who
share the Good News of Jesus with joyful exuberance.
Be such a woman. The world desperately needs your
enthusiasm—and your testimony—now!

One can never consent to creep when one feels an
impulse to soar.

Helen Keller

We must go out and live among them, manifesting
the gentle, loving spirit of our Lord. We need to make
friends before we can hope to make converts.

Lottie Moon

A WOMAN OF PRAYER

Rejoice always, pray without ceasing, in everything give thanks; for this is the will of God in Christ Jesus for you.
1 Thessalonians 5:16-18 NKJV

On his second missionary journey, Paul started a small church in Thessalonica. A short time later, he penned a letter that was intended to encourage the new believers at that church. Today, almost 2,000 years later, 1 Thessalonians remains a powerful, practical guide for Christian living.

In his letter, Paul advised members of the new church to "pray without ceasing." His advice applies to Christians of every generation. When we consult God on an hourly basis, we avail ourselves of His wisdom, His strength, and His love. As Corrie ten Boom observed, "Any concern that is too small to be turned into a prayer is too small to be made into a burden."

Today, make yourself a woman of prayer. Instead of turning things over in your mind, turn them over to God in prayer. Instead of worrying about your next decision, ask God to lead the way. Don't limit your prayers to meals or bedtime. Become a woman of constant prayer. God is listening, and He wants to hear from you. Now.

The manifold rewards of a serious, consistent prayer life demonstrate clearly that time with our Lord should be our first priority.

Shirley Dobson

QUALITY TIME, QUANTITY TIME

So teach us to number our days, that we may gain a heart of wisdom.

Psalm 90:12 NKJV

Make no mistake: caring for your family requires time—lots of time. You've probably heard about "quality time" and "quantity time." Your family needs both. So, as a responsible Christian, you should willingly invest large quantities of your time and energy in the care and nurturing of your clan.

While caring for your family, you should do your best to ensure that God remains squarely at the center of your household. When you do, God will bless you and yours in ways that you could have scarcely imagined.

———————

There is so much compassion and understanding that is gained when we've experienced God's grace firsthand within our own families.

Lisa Whelchel

Life's unfolding stops for no one.

Kathy Troccoli

YOUR BODY, GOD'S TEMPLE

Don't you know that you are God's temple and that God's Spirit lives in you?

1 Corinthians 3:16 NCV

Are you shaping up or spreading out? Do you eat sensibly and exercise regularly, or do you spend most of your time on the couch with a snack in one hand and a clicker in the other? Are you choosing to treat your body like a temple or a trash heap? How you answer these questions will help determine how long you live and how well you live.

Physical fitness is a choice, a choice that requires discipline—it's as simple as that. So, do yourself this favor: treat your body like a one-of-a-kind gift from God . . . because that's precisely what your body is.

Our primary motivation should not be for more energy or to avoid a heart attack but to please God with our bodies.

Carole Lewis

God made you a complex, interrelated being, fully integrated and interdependent.

Dr. Jordan S. Rubin

FINDING FULFILLMENT

For You, O God, have tested us; You have refined us as silver is refined . . . we went through fire and through water; but You brought us out to rich fulfillment.

Psalm 66:10–12 NKJV

Everywhere we turn, or so it seems, the world promises fulfillment, contentment, and happiness. But the contentment that the world offers is fleeting and incomplete. Thankfully, the fulfillment that God offers is all encompassing and everlasting.

Sometimes, amid the inevitable hustle and bustle of life-here-on-earth, we can forfeit—albeit temporarily—the joy of Christ as we wrestle with the challenges of daily living. Yet God's Word is clear: fulfillment through Christ is available to all who seek it and claim it. Count yourself among that number. Seek first a personal, transforming relationship with Jesus, and then claim the joy, the fulfillment, and the spiritual abundance that the Shepherd offers His sheep.

In serving we uncover the greatest fulfillment within and become a stellar example of a woman who knows and loves Jesus.

Vonette Bright

HIS GENEROSITY . . .
AND YOURS

But God demonstrates his own love for us in this: While we were still sinners, Christ died for us.

Romans 5:8 NIV

Christ showed His love for us by willingly sacrificing His own life so that we might have eternal life. We, as Christ's followers, are challenged to share His love. And, when we walk each day with Jesus—and obey the commandments found in God's Holy Word—we are worthy ambassadors for Him.

Just as Christ has been—and will always be—the ultimate friend to His flock, so should we be Christ-like in our love and generosity to those in need. When we share the love of Christ, we share a priceless gift. As His servants, we must do no less.

———

The measure of a life, after all, is not its duration but its donation.

Corrie ten Boom

The Lord has abundantly blessed me all of my life. I'm not trying to pay Him back for all of His wonderful gifts; I just realize that He gave them to me to give away.

Lisa Whelchel

HIS COMFORTING HAND

God, who comforts the downcast, comforted us . . . .
2 Corinthians 7:6 NIV

If you have been touched by the transforming hand of Jesus, then you have every reason to live courageously. Still, even if you are a dedicated Christian, you may find yourself discouraged by the inevitable disappointments and tragedies that occur in the lives of believers and non-believers alike.

The next time you find your courage tested to the limit, lean upon God's promises. Trust His Son. Remember that God is always near and that He is your protector and your deliverer. When you are worried, anxious, or afraid, call upon Him and accept the touch of His comforting hand. Remember that God rules both mountaintops and valleys—with limitless wisdom and love—now and forever.

Put your hand into the hand of God. He gives the calmness and serenity of heart and soul.

Mrs. Charles E. Cowman

A PRAYER

Dear Lord, thank You for Your comfort. You lift me up when I am disappointed. You protect me in times of trouble. Today, I will be mindful of Your love, Your wisdom, and Your grace. Amen

DISCOVERING GOD'S PLANS

It is God who is at work in you, both to will and to work for His good pleasure.

Philippians 2:13 NASB

If you seek to live in accordance with God's will for your life—and you should—then you will live in accordance with His commandments. You will study God's Word, and you will be watchful for His signs. You will associate with fellow Christians who will encourage your spiritual growth, and you will listen to that inner voice that speaks to you in the quiet moments of your daily devotionals.

God intends to use you in wonderful, unexpected ways if you let Him. The decision to seek God's plan and to follow it is yours and yours alone. The consequences of that decision have implications that are both profound and eternal, so choose carefully.

With God, it's never "Plan B" or "second best." It's always "Plan A." And, if we let Him, He'll make something beautiful of our lives.

Gloria Gaither

If God's Word, your circumstances, and the counsel of others line up, and if you sense his provision, I'd say go for it.

Luci Swindoll

STRENGTH FOR TODAY

I can do all things through Christ which strengtheneth me.

Philippians 4:13 KJV

Have you made God the cornerstone of your life, or is He relegated to a few hours on Sunday morning? Have you genuinely allowed God to reign over every corner of your heart, or have you attempted to place Him in a spiritual compartment? The answer to these questions will determine the direction of your day and your life.

God loves you. In times of trouble, He will comfort you; in times of sorrow, He will dry your tears. When you are weak or sorrowful, God is as near as your next breath. He stands at the door of your heart and waits. Welcome Him in and allow Him to rule. And then, accept the peace and the strength and the protection, and the abundance that only God can give.

In my weakness, I have learned, like Moses, to lean hard on God. The weaker I am, the harder I lean on Him. The harder I lean, the stronger I discover Him to be. The stronger I discover God to be, the more resolute I am in this job He's given me to do.

Joni Eareckson Tada

LIGHTING THE PATH

Your word is a lamp to my feet and a light to my path.
Psalm 119:105 NKJV

Are you a woman who trusts God's Word without reservation? Hopefully so, because the Bible is unlike any other book—it is a guidebook for life here on earth and for life eternal. The Psalmist describes God's Word as, "a light to my path." Is the Bible your lamp? If not, you are depriving yourself of a priceless gift from the Creator.

Vance Havner observed, "It takes calm, thoughtful, prayerful meditation on the Word to extract its deepest nourishment." How true. God's Word can be a light to guide your steps. Claim it as your light today, tomorrow, and every day of your life—and then walk confidently in the footsteps of God's only begotten Son.

One of the greatest ways God changes me is by bringing Scripture to mind that I have hidden deep in my heart. And, He always picks the right Scripture at the right time.

Evelyn Christianson

Light is stronger than darkness—darkness cannot "comprehend" or "overcome" it.

Anne Graham Lotz

NEIGHBORS IN NEED

Each one of us needs to look after the good of the people around us, asking ourselves, "How can I help?" That's exactly what Jesus did.

Romans 15:2-3 MSG

Neighbors. We know that we are instructed to love them, and yet there's so little time . . . and we're so busy. No matter. As Christians, we are commanded by our Lord and Savior Jesus Christ to love our neighbors just as we love ourselves. Period.

This very day, you will encounter someone who needs a word of encouragement or a pat on the back or a helping hand or a heartfelt prayer. And, if you don't reach out to your friend, who will? If you don't take the time to understand the needs of your neighbors, who will? If you don't love your brothers and sisters, who will? So, today, look for a neighbor in need . . . and then do something to help. Father's orders.

―――――――

No matter how crazy or nutty your life has seemed, God can make something strong and good out of it. He can help you grow wide branches for others to use as shelter.

Barbara Johnson

A LIFE OF INTEGRITY

The godly walk with integrity; blessed are their children after them.

Proverbs 20:7 NLT

Wise women understand that integrity is a crucial building block in the foundation of a well-lived life. Integrity is built slowly over a lifetime. It is the sum of every right decision, every honest word, every noble thought, and every heartfelt prayer. It is forged on the anvil of honorable work and polished by the twin virtues of generosity and humility. Integrity is a precious thing—difficult to build, but easy to tear down; godly women value it and protect it at all costs.

As believers in Christ, we must seek to live each day with discipline, honesty, and faith. When we do, at least two things happen: integrity becomes a habit, and God blesses us because of our obedience to Him.

God never called us to naïveté. He called us to integrity . . . . The biblical concept of integrity emphasizes mature innocence not childlike ignorance.

Beth Moore

A PRAYER

Heavenly Father, help me live a life of integrity. Let my words be true, and let my actions lead others to You. Amen

GOD'S LESSONS

*Take good counsel and accept correction—that's the way
to live wisely and well.*

Proverbs 19:20 MSG

When it comes to learning life's lessons, we can
either do things the easy way or the hard way. The
easy way can be summed up as follows: when God
teaches us a lesson, we learn it . . . the first time!
Unfortunately, too many of us learn much more
slowly than that.

When we resist God's instruction, He continues
to teach, whether we like it or not. Our challenge,
then, is to discern God's lessons from the experiences
of everyday life. Hopefully, we learn those lessons
sooner rather than later because the sooner we do,
the sooner He can move on to the next lesson and
the next and the next . . .

———————

True learning can take place at every age of life, and
it doesn't have to be in the curriculum plan.

Suzanne Dale Ezell

While chastening is always difficult, if we look to God
for the lesson we should learn, we will see spiritual
fruit.

Vonette Bright

THE WISDOM OF MODERATION

Moderation is better than muscle, self-control better than political power.

Proverbs 16:32 MSG

Moderation and wisdom are traveling companions. If we are wise, we must learn to temper our appetites, our desires, and our impulses. When we do, we are blessed, in part, because God has created a world in which temperance is rewarded and intemperance is inevitably punished.

Would you like to improve your life? Then harness your appetites and restrain your impulses. Moderation is difficult, of course; it is especially difficult in a prosperous society such as ours. But the rewards of moderation are numerous and long-lasting. Claim those rewards today. No one can force you to moderate your appetites. The decision to live temperately (and wisely) is yours and yours alone. And so are the consequences.

When I feel like circumstances are spiraling downward in my life, God taught me that whether I'm right side up or upside down, I need to turn those circumstances over to Him. He is the only one who can bring balance into my life.

Carole Lewis

OPTIMISM 101

I can do everything through him that gives me strength.
Philippians 4:13 NIV

Pessimism and Christianity don't mix. Why? Because Christians have every reason to be optimistic about life here on earth and life eternal. Mrs. Charles E. Cowman advised, "Never yield to gloomy anticipation. Place your hope and confidence in God. He has no record of failure."

Sometimes, despite our trust in God, we may fall into the spiritual traps of worry, frustration, anxiety, or sheer exhaustion, and our hearts become heavy. What's needed is plenty of rest, a large dose of perspective, and God's healing touch, but not necessarily in that order. So, make this promise to yourself and keep it: vow to be a hope-filled Christian. Think optimistically about your life, your profession, and your future. Trust your hopes, not your fears. Take time to celebrate God's glorious creation. And then, when you've filled your heart with hope and gladness, share your optimism with others. They'll be better for it, and so will you. But not necessarily in that order.

If you can't tell whether your glass is half-empty or half-full, you don't need another glass; what you need is better eyesight . . . and a more thankful heart.

Marie T. Freeman

WITH GOD'S STRENGTH

Come to Me, all you who are weary and burdened, and I will give you rest. Take My yoke upon you and learn from Me, because I am gentle and humble in heart, and you will find rest for your souls. For My yoke is easy and My burden is light.

Matthew 11:28–30 HCSB

Are you tired? Ask God for strength. Are you discouraged? Believe in His promises. Are you frustrated or fearful? Pray as if everything depended upon God, and work as if everything depended upon you. With God's help, you will find the strength to be the kind of woman who makes your Heavenly Father beam with pride.

Perhaps you are in a hurry for God to reveal His plans for your life. If so, be forewarned: God operates on His own timetable, not yours. Sometimes, God may answer your prayers with silence, and when He does, you must patiently persevere. In times of trouble, you must remain steadfast and trust in the merciful goodness of your Heavenly Father. Whatever your problem, He can handle it. Your job is to keep persevering until He does.

If things are tough, remember that every flower that ever bloomed had to go through a whole lot of dirt to get there.

Barbara Johnson

NOW, NOT LATER

We can't afford to waste a minute, must not squander these precious daylight hours in frivolity and indulgence . . . . Don't loiter and linger, waiting until the very last minute. Dress yourselves in Christ, and be up and about!

Romans 13:13-14 MSG

The habit of procrastination takes a two-fold toll on its victims. First, important work goes unfinished; second (and more importantly), valuable energy is wasted in the process of putting off the things that remain undone. Procrastination results from an individual's short-sighted attempt to postpone temporary discomfort. What results is a senseless cycle of 1. delay, followed by 2. worry followed by 3. a panicky and often futile attempt to "catch up." Procrastination is, at its core, a struggle against oneself; the only antidote is action.

Once you acquire the habit of doing what needs to be done when it needs to be done, you will avoid untold trouble, worry, and stress. So learn to defeat procrastination by paying less attention to your fears and more attention to your responsibilities. God has created a world that punishes procrastinators and rewards women who "do it now." Life doesn't procrastinate—neither should you.

Never fail to do something because you don't feel like it. Sometimes you just have to do it now, and you'll feel like it later.

Marie T. Freeman

THE POWER OF WORDS

The wise don't tell everything they know, but the foolish talk too much and are ruined.

Proverbs 10:14 NCV

All too often, in the rush to have ourselves heard, we speak first and think next . . . with unfortunate results. God's Word reminds us that, "Reckless words pierce like a sword, but the tongue of the wise brings healing" (Proverbs 12:18 NIV). If we seek to be a source of encouragement to friends and family, then we must measure our words carefully. Words are important: they can hurt or heal. Words can uplift us or discourage us, and reckless words, spoken in haste, cannot be erased.

Today, measure your words carefully. Use words of kindness and praise, not words of anger or derision. Remember that you have the power to heal others or to injure them, to lift others up or to hold them back. When you lift them up, your wisdom will bring healing and comfort to a world that needs both.

The battle of the tongue is won not in the mouth, but in the heart.

Annie Chapman

A PRAYER

Dear Lord, keep me mindful that I have influence on many people. Let the words that I speak today be worthy of the One who has saved me forever. Amen

YOUR WAY OR GOD'S WAY

A man's heart plans his way, but the Lord directs his steps.

Proverbs 16:9 NKJV

The popular song "My Way" is a perfectly good tune, but it's not a perfect guide for life-here-on-earth. If you're looking for life's perfect prescription, you'd better forget about doing things your way and start doing things God's way. The most important decision of your life is, of course, your commitment to accept Jesus Christ as your personal Lord and Savior. And once your eternal destiny is secured, you will undoubtedly ask yourself the question "What now, Lord?" If you earnestly seek God's will for your life, you will find it . . . in time.

Sometimes, God's plans are crystal clear; sometimes they are not. So be patient, keep searching, and keep praying. If you do, then in time, God will answer your prayers and make His plans known. You'll discover those plans by doing things His way . . . and you'll be eternally grateful that you did.

We cannot always understand the ways of Almighty God—the crosses which he sends us, the sacrifices which he demands of us. But, if we accept with faith and resignation his holy will—with no looking back to what might have been—we are at peace.

Rose Fitzgerald Kennedy

TRUSTING HIM COMPLETELY

I will be your God throughout your lifetime—until your hair is white with age. I made you, and I will care for you. I will carry you along and save you.

Isaiah 46:4 NLT

God has promised to lift you up and guide your steps if you let Him do so. God has promised that when you entrust your life to Him completely and without reservation, He will give you the strength to meet any challenge, the courage to face any trial, and the wisdom to live in His righteousness.

God's hand uplifts those who turn their hearts and prayers to Him. Will you count yourself among that number? Will you accept God's peace and wear God's armor against the temptations and distractions of our dangerous world? If you do, you can live courageously and optimistically, knowing that you have been forever touched by the loving, unfailing, uplifting hand of God.

Snuggle in God's arms. When you are hurting, when you feel lonely or left out, let Him cradle you, comfort you, reassure you of His all-sufficient power and love.

Kay Arthur

When we trust the author, we don't have to know the story. We just know it will be true.

Gloria Gaither

A FEARLESS WOMAN

Teach me Your way, O Lord; I will walk in Your truth.
Psalm 86:11 NKJV

The Book of Judges (chapters 4 and 5) tells the story of Deborah, the fearless woman who helped lead the army of Israel to victory over the Canaanites. Deborah was a judge and a prophetess, a woman called by God to lead her people. And when she answered God's call, she was rewarded with one of the great victories of Old Testament times. Like Deborah, all of us are called to serve our Creator. And, like Deborah, we may sometimes find ourselves facing trials that can bring trembling to the very depths of our souls. As believers, we must seek God's will and follow it.

As this day unfolds, seek God's will for your own life and obey His Word. He will give you the strength to meet any challenge, the courage to face any trial, and the wisdom to live in His righteousness and in His peace.

Fear is a strange wind. It is not a wind that propels us forward, but a wild paralyzing one that puts us in a holding pattern. We can't move. We can't fly backward or forward. We are stuck, held fast.

Sheila Walsh

FILLED WITH THE SPIRIT

Do not be drunk with wine, which will ruin you, but be filled with the Spirit.

Ephesians 5:18 NCV

When you are filled with the Holy Spirit, your words and deeds will reflect a love and devotion to Christ. When you are filled with the Holy Spirit, the steps of your life's journey are guided by the Lord. When you allow God's Spirit to work in you and through you, you will be energized and transformed.

Today, allow yourself to be filled with the Spirit of God. And then stand back in amazement as God begins to work miracles in your own life and in the lives of those you love.

The Holy Spirit is like a living and continually flowing fountain in believers. We have the boundless privilege of tapping into that fountain every time we pray.

Shirley Dobson

The Holy Spirit testifies of Jesus. So when you are filled with the Holy Spirit you speak about our Lord and really live to His honor.

Corrie ten Boom

THE WORLD'S BEST FRIEND

Greater love has no one than this, that he lay down his life for his friends.

John 15:13 NIV

Who's the best friend this world has ever had? Jesus, of course. When you invite Him into your heart, Jesus will be your friend, too . . . your friend forever. Jesus has offered to share the gifts of everlasting life and everlasting love with the world . . . and with you. If you make mistakes, He'll still be your friend. If you behave badly, He'll still love you. If you feel sorry or sad, He will help you feel better about your world and yourself.

Jesus wants you to have a happy, meaningful life. He wants you to be generous and kind, and He wants you to follow Him. The rest, of course, is up to you. You can do it! And with a friend like Jesus, you most certainly will.

When we are in a situation where Jesus is all we have, we soon discover he is all we really need.

Gigi Graham Tchividjian

Tell me the story of Jesus. Write on my heart every word. Tell me the story most precious, sweetest that ever was heard.

Fanny Crosby

TOO MANY POSSESSIONS

Do not love the world or the things in the world. If you love the world, the love of the Father is not in you.

1 John 2:15 NCV

On the grand stage of a well-lived life, material possessions should play a rather small role. Of course, we all need the basic necessities of life, but once we meet those needs for ourselves and for our families, the piling up of possessions creates more problems than it solves. Our real riches, of course, are not of this world. We are never really rich until we are rich in spirit.

How much stuff is too much stuff? Well, if your desire for stuff is getting in the way of your desire to know God, then you've got too much stuff—it's as simple as that. So, if you find yourself wrapped up in the concerns of the material world, it's time to reorder your priorities. And, it's time to begin storing up riches that will endure throughout eternity—the spiritual kind.

We own too many things that aren't worth owning.

Marie T. Freeman

The more we stuff ourselves with material pleasures, the less we seem to appreciate life.

Barbara Johnson

ON A MISSION

You are a chosen people. You are a kingdom of priests, God's holy nation, his very own possession. This is so you can show others the goodness of God, for he called you out of the darkness into his wonderful light.

1 Peter 2:9 NLT

Whether you realize it or not, you are on a personal mission for God. As a Christian, that mission is straightforward: Honor God, accept Christ as your personal Savior, and serve God's children.

Of course, you will encounter impediments as you attempt to discover the exact nature of God's purpose for your life, but you must never lose sight of the overriding purposes that God has established for all believers. You will encounter these overriding purposes again and again as you worship your Creator and study His Word.

Every day offers countless opportunities to serve God and to worship Him. When you do so, He will bless you in miraculous ways. May you continue to seek God's will, may you trust His word, and may you place Him where He belongs: at the very center of your life.

I am more and more persuaded that all that is required of us is faithful seed-sowing. The harvest is bound to follow.

Annie Armstrong

GOD'S GUIDANCE AND YOUR PATH

Trust in the LORD with all your heart; do not depend on your own understanding. Seek his will in all you do, and he will direct your paths.

Proverbs 3:5-6 NLT

Proverbs 3:5-6 makes this promise: if you acknowledge God's sovereignty over every aspect of your life, He will guide your path. And, as you prayerfully consider the path that God intends for you to take, here are things you should do: You should study His Word and be ever-watchful for His signs. You should associate with fellow believers who will encourage your spiritual growth. You should listen carefully to that inner voice that speaks to you in the quiet moments of your daily devotionals. And you should be patient. Your Heavenly Father may not always reveal Himself as quickly as you would like, but rest assured that God intends to use you in wonderful, unexpected ways. Your challenge is to watch, to listen, to learn . . . and to follow.

If you are God's child, you are no longer bound to your past or to what you were. You are a brand new creature in Christ Jesus.

Kay Arthur

THE POWER OF PRAYER

The intense prayer of the righteous is very powerful.
James 5:16 HCSB

"The power of prayer": these words are so familiar, yet sometimes we forget what they mean. Prayer is a powerful tool for communicating with our Creator; it is an opportunity to commune with the Giver of all things good. Prayer helps us find strength for today and hope for the future. Prayer is not a thing to be taken lightly or to be used infrequently.

The quality of your spiritual life will be in direct proportion to the quality of your prayer life. Prayer changes things, and it changes you. Today, instead of turning things over in your mind, turn them over to God in prayer. Instead of worrying about your next decision, ask God to lead the way. Pray constantly about things great and small. God is listening, and He wants to hear from you now.

The greatest power that God has given to any individual is the power of prayer.

Kathryn Kuhlman

Always stay connected to people and seek out things that bring you joy. Dream with abandon. Pray confidently.

Barbara Johnson

A QUIET PLACE

Now in the morning, having risen a long while before daylight, He went out and departed to a solitary place; and there He prayed.

Mark 1:35 NKJV

In the first chapter of Mark, we read that in the darkness of the early morning hours, Jesus went to a solitary place and prayed. So, too, should we. But sometimes, finding quiet moments of solitude is difficult indeed. We live in a noisy world, a world filled with distractions, frustrations, and complications. But if we allow the distractions of a clamorous world to separate us from God's peace, we do ourselves a profound disservice. Are you one of those busy women who rush through the day with scarcely a single moment for quiet contemplation and prayer? If so, it's time to reorder your priorities. Nothing is more important than the time you spend with your Savior. So be still and claim the inner peace that is your spiritual birthright: the peace of Jesus Christ.

The more complicated life becomes, the more we need to quiet our souls before God.

Elisabeth Elliot

SO MANY TEMPTATIONS

But remember that the temptations that come into your life are no different from what others experience. And God is faithful. He will keep the temptation from becoming so strong that you can't stand up against it. When you are tempted, he will show you a way out so that you will not give in to it.

1 Corinthians 10:13 NLT

This world is filled to the brim with temptations. Some of these temptations are small; eating a second scoop of ice cream, for example, is tempting, but not very dangerous. Other temptations, however, are not nearly so harmless. The devil is working 24/7, and he's causing pain and heartache in more ways than ever before. Thankfully, in the battle against Satan, we are never alone. God is always with us, and He gives us the power to resist temptation whenever we ask Him for the strength to do so.

In a letter to believers, Peter offered a stern warning: "Your adversary, the devil, prowls around like a roaring lion, seeking someone to devour" (1 Peter 5:8 NASB). As Christians, we must take that warning seriously, and we must behave accordingly.

The devil's most devilish when respectable.

Elizabeth Barrett Browning

DOERS OF THE WORD

But prove yourselves doers of the word, and not merely hearers.

James 1:22 NASB

The old saying is both familiar and true: actions speak louder than words. And as believers, we must beware: our actions should always give credence to the changes that Christ can make in the lives of those who walk with Him.

God calls upon each of us to act in accordance with His will and with respect for His commandments. If we are to be responsible believers, we must realize that it is never enough simply to hear the instructions of God; we must also live by them. And it is never enough to wait idly by while others do God's work here on earth; we, too, must act. Doing God's work is a responsibility that each of us must bear, and when we do, our loving Heavenly Father rewards our efforts with a bountiful harvest.

From the very moment one feels called to act is born the strength to bear whatever horror one will feel or see. In some inexplicable way, terror loses its overwhelming power when it becomes a task that must be faced.

Emmi Bonhoeffer

FORGIVENESS STARTS AT HOME

Let all bitterness, wrath, anger, clamor, and evil speaking be put away from you, with all malice. And be kind to one another, tenderhearted, forgiving one another, just as God in Christ forgave you.

Ephesians 4:31-32 NKJV

Sometimes, it's easy to become angry with the people we love most, and sometimes it's hard to forgive them. After all, we know that our family will still love us no matter how angry we become. But while it's easy to become angry at home, it's usually wrong.

The next time you're tempted to lose your temper or to remain angry at a close family member, ask God to help you find the wisdom to forgive. And while you're at it, do your best to calm down sooner rather than later because peace is always beautiful, especially when it's peace at your house.

———————————

There is no sin nor wrong that gives a man such a foretaste of hell in this life as anger and impatience.

St. Catherine of Siena

FACING FEARS,
LIVING BOLDLY

God doesn't want us to be shy with his gifts, but bold and loving and sensible.

2 Timothy 1:7 MSG

Do you prefer to face your fears rather than run from them? If so, you will be blessed because of your willingness to live courageously.

When Paul wrote Timothy, he reminded his young protégé that the God they served was a bold God, and God's spirit empowered His children with boldness also. Like Timothy, we face times of uncertainty and fear. God's message is the same to us, today, as it was to Timothy: We can live boldly because the spirit of God resides in us.

So today, as you face the challenges of everyday living, remember that God is with you . . . and you are protected.

The pathway of obedience can sometimes be difficult, but it always leads to a strengthening of our inner woman.

Vonette Bright

God did away with all my fear. It was time for someone to stand up—or in my case, sit down. So I refused to move.

Rosa Parks

THE PURSUIT
OF GOD'S TRUTH

But grow in the grace and knowledge of our Lord and Savior Jesus Christ. To Him be the glory both now and forever. Amen.

2 Peter 3:18 NKJV

Have you established a passionate relationship with God's Holy Word? Hopefully so. After all, the Bible is a roadmap for life here on earth and for life eternal. And, as a believer who has been touched by God's grace, you are called upon to study God's Holy Word, to trust His Word, to follow its commandments, and to share its Good News with the world.

The words of Matthew 4:4 remind us that, "Man shall not live by bread alone but by every word that proceedeth out of the mouth of God" (KJV). As believers, we must study the Bible and meditate upon its meaning for our lives. Otherwise, we deprive ourselves of a priceless gift from our Creator. God's Holy Word is, indeed, a transforming gift from the Father in heaven. That's why passionate believers must never live by bread alone . . .

———————————

We can't stand before God on the day of judgment and explain that our incredible ignorance is our pastor's fault. It is our responsibility to access God's Word for ourselves.

Sheila Walsh

CELEBRATION WITH A SMILE

Jacob said, "For what a relief it is to see your friendly smile. It is like seeing the smile of God!"

Genesis 33:10 NLT

Life should never be taken for granted. Each day is a priceless gift from God and should be treated as such.

Hannah Whitall Smith observed, "How changed our lives would be if we could only fly through the days on wings of surrender and trust!" How true!

Today, let us celebrate life with smiles on our faces and kind words on our lips. After all, this is God's day, and He has given us clear instructions for its use. We are commanded to rejoice and be glad. So, with no further ado, let the celebration begin . . .

Friendship fills a deep well within me with fresh water. When I celebrate my friendships, it's like dropping a huge rock into the well. It splashes that water everywhere, on everyone else in my life.

Nicole Johnson

Let no one ever come to you without leaving better and happier. Be the living expression of God's kindness: kindness in your face, kindness in your eyes, kindness in your smile.

Mother Teresa

UNBENDING TRUTH

So put away all falsehood and "tell your neighbor the truth" because we belong to each other.

Ephesians 4:25 NLT

We live in a world that presents us with countless temptations to wander far from God's path. These temptations have the potential to destroy us, in part, because they cause us to be dishonest with ourselves and with others. Dishonesty is a habit. Once we start bending the truth, we're likely to keep bending it. A far better strategy, of course, is to acquire the habit of being completely forthright with God, with other people, and with ourselves.

Honesty is also a habit, a habit that pays powerful dividends for those who place character above convenience. So, the next time you're tempted to bend the truth—or to break it—ask yourself this simple question: "What does God want to do?" Then listen carefully to your conscience. When you do, your actions will be honorable, and your character will take care of itself.

Character cannot be developed in ease and quiet. Only through experience of trial and suffering can the soul be strengthened, vision cleared, ambition inspired, and success achieved.

Helen Keller

SAYING YES TO GOD

Fear thou not; for I am with thee.

Isaiah 41:10 KJV

Your decision to seek a deeper relationship with God will not remove all problems from your life; to the contrary, it will bring about a series of personal crises as you constantly seek to say "yes" to God although the world encourages you to do otherwise. Each time you are tempted to distance yourself from the Creator, you will face a spiritual crisis. A few of these crises may be monumental in scope, but most will be the small, everyday decisions of life. In fact, life here on earth can be seen as one test after another—and with each crisis comes yet another opportunity to grow closer to God . . . or to distance yourself from His plan for your life.

Today, you will face many opportunities to say "yes" to your Creator—and you will also encounter many opportunities to say "no" to Him. Your answers will determine the quality of your day and the direction of your life, so answer carefully . . . very carefully.

The Christian lifestyle is not one of legalistic do's and don'ts, but one that is positive, attractive, and joyful.

Vonette Bright

COMFORTING OTHERS

Carry each other's burdens, and in this way you will fulfill the law of Christ.

Galatians 6:2 NIV

We live in a world that is, on occasion, a frightening place. Sometimes, we sustain life-altering losses that are so profound and so tragic that it seems we could never recover. But, with God's help and with the help of encouraging family members and friends, we can recover.

In times of need, God's Word is clear: as believers, we must offer comfort to those in need by sharing not only our courage but also our faith. As the revivalist Vance Havner observed, "No journey is complete that does not lead through some dark valleys. We can properly comfort others only with the comfort wherewith we ourselves have been comforted of God." Enough said.

———

So often we think that to be encouragers we have to produce great words of wisdom when, in fact, a few simple syllables of sympathy and an arm around the shoulder can often provide much needed comfort.

Florence Littauer

CONTENTMENT THAT LASTS

Serving God does make us very rich, if we are satisfied with what we have. We brought nothing into the world, so we can take nothing out. But, if we have food and clothes, we will be satisfied with that.

1 Timothy 6:6–8 NCV

The preoccupation with happiness and contentment is an ever-present theme in the modern world. We are bombarded with messages that tell us where to find peace and pleasure in a world that worships materialism and wealth. But, lasting contentment is not found in material possessions; genuine contentment is a spiritual gift from God to those who trust in Him and follow His commandments. When God dwells at the center of our lives, peace and contentment will belong to us just as surely as we belong to God.

If I could just hang in there, being faithful to my own tasks, God would make me joyful and content. The responsibility is mine, but the power is His.

Peg Rankin

The key to contentment is to consider. Consider who you are and be satisfied with that. Consider what you have and be satisfied with that. Consider what God's doing and be satisfied with that.

Luci Swindoll

ENOUGH HOURS
IN THE DAY?

It is good to give thanks to the Lord, to sing praises to the Most High. It is good to proclaim your unfailing love in the morning, your faithfulness in the evening.

Psalm 92:1-2 NLT

Each day has 1,440 minutes—do you value your relationship with God enough to spend a few of those minutes with Him? He deserves that much of your time and more—is He receiving it from you? Hopefully so. But if you find that you're simply "too busy" for a daily chat with your Father in heaven, it's time to take a long, hard look at your priorities and your values.

As you consider your plans for the day ahead, here's a tip: organize your life around this simple principle: "God first." When you place your Creator where He belongs—at the very center of your day and your life—the rest of your priorities will fall into place.

Knowing God involves an intimate, personal relationship that is developed over time through prayer and getting answers to prayer, through Bible study and applying its teaching to our lives, through obedience and experiencing the power of God, through moment-by-moment submission to Him that results in a moment-by-moment filling of the Holy Spirit.

Anne Graham Lotz

DOUBT AND BELIEF

Immediately the father of the child cried out and said with tears, "Lord, I believe; help my unbelief!"

Mark 9:24 NKJV

Even the most faithful Christians are overcome by occasional bouts of fear and doubt. You are no different. When you feel that your faith is being tested to its limits, seek the comfort and assurance of the One who sent His Son as a sacrifice for you.

Have you ever felt your faith in God slipping away? If so, you are not alone. Every life—including yours—is a series of successes and failures, celebrations and disappointments, joys and sorrows, hopes and doubts. But even when you feel very distant from God, God is never distant from you. When you sincerely seek His presence, He will touch your heart, calm your fears, and restore your faith in the future, and your faith in Him.

To wrestle with God does not mean that we have lost faith, but that we are fighting for it.

Sheila Walsh

A PRAYER

Dear Lord, when I am filled with uncertainty and doubt, give me faith. In the dark moments of life, keep me mindful of Your healing power and Your infinite love, so that I may live courageously and faithfully today and every day. Amen

THE POWER OF OUR WORDS

Watch the way you talk. Let nothing foul or dirty come out of your mouth. Say only what helps, each word a gift.

Ephesians 4:29 MSG

The words that we speak have the power to do great good or great harm. If we speak words of encouragement and hope, we can lift others up. And that's exactly what God commands us to do!

Sometimes, when we feel uplifted and secure, it is easy to speak kind words. Other times, when we are discouraged or tired, we can scarcely summon the energy to uplift ourselves, much less anyone else. God intends that we speak words of kindness, wisdom, and truth, no matter our circumstances, no matter our emotions. When we do, we share a priceless gift with the world, and we give glory to the One who gave His life for us. As believers, we must do no less.

If someone listens or stretches out a hand or whispers a word of encouragement or attempts to understand a lonely person, extraordinary things begin to happen.

Loretta Girzartis

Every word we speak, every action we take, has an effect on the totality of humanity. No one can escape that privilege—or that responsibility.

Laurie Beth Jones

CHOOSING THE GOOD LIFE

And in that day you will ask Me nothing. Most assuredly, I say to you, whatever you ask the Father in My name He will give you. Until now you have asked nothing in My name. Ask, and you will receive, that your joy may be full.

John 16:23-24 NKJV

God offers us abundance through His Son, Jesus. Whether or not we accept God's abundance is, of course, up to each of us. When we entrust our hearts and our days to the One who created us, we experience abundance through the grace and sacrifice of His Son, Jesus. But, when we turn our thoughts and our energies away from God's commandments, we inevitably forfeit the spiritual abundance that might otherwise be ours.

What is your focus today? Are you focused on God's Word and His will for your life? Or are you focused on the distractions and temptations of a difficult world. The answer to this question will, to a surprising extent, determine the quality and the direction of your day.

If you sincerely seek the spiritual abundance that your Savior offers, then follow Him completely and without reservation. When you do, you will receive the love, the life, and the abundance that He has promised.

WHEN ANGER IS APPROPRIATE

The face of the Lord is against those who do evil.

Psalm 34:16 NKJV

Sometimes, anger can be a good thing. In the 22nd chapter of Matthew, we see how Christ responded when He confronted the evildoings of those who invaded His Father's house of worship: "And Jesus entered the temple and drove out all those who were buying and selling in the temple, and overturned the tables of the moneychangers and the seats of those who were selling doves" (v. 12 NASB). Thus, Jesus proved that righteous indignation is an appropriate response to evil.

When you come face-to-face with the devil's handiwork, don't be satisfied to remain safely on the sidelines. Instead, follow in the footsteps of your Savior. Jesus never compromised with evil, and neither should you.

_____

When something robs you of your peace of mind, ask yourself if it is worth the energy you are expending on it. If not, then put it out of your mind in an act of discipline. Every time the thought of "it" returns, refuse it.

Kay Arthur

Anger unresolved will only bring you woe.

Kay Arthur

ASKING AND RECEIVING

Ask, and it will be given to you; seek, and you will find; knock, and it will be opened to you. For everyone who asks receives, and he who seeks finds, and to him who knocks it will be opened.

Matthew 7:7-8 NKJV

Are you a woman who asks God for guidance and strength? If so, then you're continually inviting your Creator to reveal Himself in a variety of ways. As a follower of Christ, you must do no less.

Jesus made it clear to His disciples: they should petition God to meet their needs. So should we. Genuine, heartfelt prayer produces powerful changes in us and in our world. When we lift our hearts to God, we open ourselves to a never-ending source of divine wisdom and infinite love.

Whatever your need, no matter how great or small, pray about it and never lose hope. God is not just near; He is here, and He's perfectly capable of answering your prayers. Now, it's up to you to ask.

––––––––

God makes prayer as easy as possible for us. He's completely approachable and available, and He'll never mock or upbraid us for bringing our needs before Him.

Shirley Dobson

RIGHTEOUSNESS NOW!

By this we know that we have come to know Him, if we keep His commandments.

1 John 2:3 NASB

When we seek righteousness in our own lives—and when we seek the companionship of those who do likewise—we reap the spiritual rewards that God intends for us to enjoy. When we behave ourselves as godly women, we honor God. When we live righteously and according to God's commandments, He blesses us in ways that we cannot fully understand.

Today, as you fulfill your responsibilities, hold fast to that which is good, and associate yourself with believers who behave themselves in like fashion. When you do, your good works will serve as a powerful example for others and as a worthy offering to your Creator.

We are to leave an impression on all those we meet that communicates whose we are and what kingdom we represent.

Lisa Bevere

Let us never suppose that obedience is impossible or that holiness is meant only for a select few. Our Shepherd leads us in paths of righteousness—not for our name's sake but for His.

Elisabeth Elliot

ACKNOWLEDGING YOUR BLESSINGS

The Lord bless you and keep you; The Lord make His face shine upon you, And be gracious to you.

Numbers 6:24-25 NKJV

When the demands of life leave us rushing from place to place with scarcely a moment to spare, we may fail to pause and thank our Creator for His gifts. But, whenever we neglect to give proper thanks to the Father, we suffer because of our misplaced priorities.

Today, begin making a list of your blessings. You most certainly will not be able to make a complete list, but take a few moments and jot down as many blessings as you can. Then, give thanks to the Giver of all good things: God. His love for you is eternal, as are His gifts. And it's never too soon—or too late—to offer Him thanks.

I discovered that sorrow was not to be feared but rather endured with hope and expectancy that God would use it to visit and bless my life.

Jill Briscoe

Get rich quick! Count your blessings!

Anonymous

CHEERFUL CHRISTIANITY

Be cheerful. Keep things in good repair. Keep your spirits up. Think in harmony. Be agreeable. Do all that, and the God of love and peace will be with you for sure.

2 Corinthians 13:11 MSG

Mrs. Charles E. Cowman, the author of the classic devotional text, *Streams in the Desert*, wrote, "Two wings are necessary to lift our souls toward God: prayer and praise. Prayer asks. Praise accepts the answer." That's why we should find the time to lift our concerns to God in prayer, and to praise Him for all that He has done. John Wesley correctly observed, "Sour godliness is the devil's religion." His words remind us that pessimism and doubt are some of the most important tools that Satan uses to achieve his objectives. Our challenge, of course, is to ensure that Satan cannot use these tools on us.

Are you a cheerful Christian? You should be! And what is the best way to attain the joy that is rightfully yours? By giving Christ what is rightfully His: your heart, your soul, and your life.

Cheerfulness prepares a glorious mind for all the noblest acts of religion—love, adoration, praise, and every union with our God.

St. Elizabeth Ann Seton

A SERIES OF CHOICES

The thing you should want most is God's kingdom and doing what God wants. Then all these other things you need will be given to you.

Matthew 6:33 NCV

Your life is a series of choices. From the instant you wake up in the morning until the moment you nod off to sleep at night, you make countless decisions—decisions about the things you do, decisions about the words you speak, and decisions about the way that you choose to direct your thoughts.

As a woman who has been transformed by the love of Jesus, you have every reason to make wise choices. But sometimes, when the daily grind threatens to grind you up and spit you out, you may make choices that are displeasing to God. When you do, you'll pay a price because you'll forfeit the happiness and the peace that might otherwise have been yours.

So, as you pause to consider the kind of Christian you are—and the kind of Christian you want to become—ask yourself whether you're sitting on the fence or standing in the light. The choice is yours . . . and so are the consequences.

I do not know how the Spirit of Christ performs it, but He brings us choices through which we constantly change, fresh and new, into His likeness.

Joni Eareckson Tada

COMPASSIONATE SERVANTS

Finally, all of you be of one mind, having compassion for one another; love as brothers, be tenderhearted, be courteous.

1 Peter 3:8 NKJV

God's Word commands us to be compassionate, generous servants to those who need our support. As believers, we have been richly blessed by our Creator. We, in turn, are called to share our gifts, our possessions, our testimonies, and our talents.

Concentration camp survivor Corrie ten Boom correctly observed, "The measure of a life is not its duration but its donation." These words remind us that the quality of our lives is determined not by what are able to take from others, but instead by what we are able to share with others.

The thread of compassion is woven into the very fabric of Christ's teachings. If we are to be disciples of Christ, we, too, must be zealous in caring for others.

———

Reach out and care for someone who needs the touch of hospitality. The time you spend caring today will be a love gift that will blossom into the fresh joy of God's Spirit in the future.

Emilie Barnes

CONFIDENT CHRISTIANITY

You are my hope; O Lord GOD, You are my confidence.

Psalm 71:5 NASB

We Christians have many reasons to be confident. God is in His heaven; Christ has risen, and we are the sheep of His flock. Yet sometimes, even the most devout Christians can become discouraged. Discouragement, however, is not God's way; He is a God of possibility not negativity.

Are you a confident Christian? You should be. God's grace is eternal and His promises are unambiguous. So count your blessings, not your hardships. And live courageously. God is the Giver of all things good, and He watches over you today and forever.

———————

As I have grown in faith and confidence, I have known more and more that my worth is based on the love of God.

Leslie Williams

A PRAYER

Lord, when I place my confidence in the things of this earth, I will be disappointed. But, when I put my confidence in You, I am secure. In every aspect of my life, Father, let me place my hope and my trust in Your infinite wisdom and Your boundless grace. Amen

CONSIDERING THE CROSS

But God forbid that I should boast except in the cross of our Lord Jesus Christ, by whom the world has been crucified to me, and I to the world.

Galatians 6:14 NKJV

As we consider Christ's sacrifice on the cross, we should be profoundly humbled and profoundly grateful. And today, as we come to Christ in prayer, we should do so in a spirit of quiet, heartfelt devotion to the One who gave His life so that we might have life eternal.

He was the Son of God, but He wore a crown of thorns. He was the Savior of mankind, yet He was put to death on a roughhewn cross made of wood. He offered His healing touch to an unsaved world, and yet the same hands that had healed the sick and raised the dead were pierced with nails.

Christ humbled Himself on a cross—for you. As you approach Him today in prayer, think about His love and His sacrifice. And be grateful.

The cross epitomizes the retribution that comes to those who give up controlling and triumphalist postures in order to relate to others in mutual love.

Sallie McFague

A WORTHY DISCIPLE

He has showed you, O man, what is good. And what does the LORD require of you? To act justly and to love mercy and to walk humbly with your God.

Micah 6:8 NIV

When Jesus addressed His disciples, He warned that each one must, "take up his cross and follow me." The disciples must have known exactly what the Master meant. In Jesus' day, prisoners were forced to carry their own crosses to the location where they would be put to death. Thus, Christ's message was clear: in order to follow Him, Christ's disciples must deny themselves and, instead, trust Him completely. Nothing has changed since then.

If we are to be disciples of Christ, we must trust Him and place Him at the very center of our beings. Jesus never comes "next." He is always first.

Do you seek to be a worthy disciple of Christ? Then pick up His cross today and every day that you live. When you do, He will bless you now and forever.

I lived with Indians who made pots out of clay which they used for cooking. Nobody was interested in the pot. Everybody was interested in what was inside. The same clay taken out of the same riverbed, always made in the same design, nothing special about it. Well, I'm a clay pot, and let me not forget it. But, the excellency of the power is of God and not us.

Elisabeth Elliot

AN INTENSELY BRIGHT
FUTURE: YOURS

I came so they can have real and eternal life, more and better life than they ever dreamed of.

John 10:10 MSG

Are you excited about the opportunities of today and thrilled by the possibilities of tomorrow? Do you confidently expect God to lead you to a place of abundance, peace, and joy? And, when your days on earth are over, do you expect to receive the priceless gift of eternal life? If you trust God's promises, and if you have welcomed God's Son into your heart, then you believe that your future is intensely and eternally bright.

It takes courage to dream big dreams. You will discover that courage when you do three things: accept the past, trust God to handle the future, and make the most of the time He has given you today. No dreams are too big for God—not even yours. So start living—and dreaming—accordingly.

You pay God a compliment by asking great things of Him.

St. Teresa of Avila

Our yesterdays teach us how to savor our todays and tomorrows.

Patsy Clairmont

WHAT KIND OF EXAMPLE?

In everything set them an example by doing what is good.

Titus 2:7 NIV

What kind of example are you? Are you the kind of woman whose life serves as a powerful example of decency and morality? Are you a woman whose behavior serves as a positive role model for others? Are you the kind of person whose actions, day in and day out, are based upon integrity, fidelity, and a love for the Lord? If so, you are not only blessed by God, you are also a powerful force for good in a world that desperately needs positive influences such as yours. And that's good because your family and friends are watching . . . and so, for that matter, is God.

––––––––––

In serving we uncover the greatest fulfillment within and become a stellar example of a woman who knows and loves Jesus.

Vonette Bright

"I read about it in the Bible" is true and good. Yet, "I have seen him with the eyes of my heart" is often more convincing. And convicting.

Liz Curtis Higgs

TEMPORARY SETBACKS

A time to weep, and a time to laugh; a time to mourn, and a time to dance . . . .

Ecclesiastes 3:4 KJV

The occasional disappointments and failures of life are inevitable. Such setbacks are simply the price that we must occasionally pay for our willingness to take risks as we follow our dreams. But even when we encounter bitter disappointments, we must never lose faith.

When we encounter the inevitable difficulties of life-here-on-earth, God stands ready to protect us. Our responsibility, of course, is to ask Him for protection. When we call upon Him in heartfelt prayer, He will answer—in His own time and according to His own plan—and He will heal us. And, while we are waiting for God's plans to unfold and for His healing touch to restore us, we can be comforted in the knowledge that our Creator can overcome any obstacle, even if we cannot.

———

Every misfortune, every failure, every loss may be transformed. God has the power to transform all misfortunes into "God-sends."

Mrs. Charles E. Cowman

FINANCIAL SECURITY

Honor the Lord with your wealth and the firstfruits from all your crops. Then your barns will be full, and your wine barrels will overflow with new wine.

Proverbs 3:9-10 NCV

The quest for financial security is a journey that leads us across many peaks and through a few unexpected valleys. When we reach the mountaintops, we find it easy to praise God and to give thanks. But, when we face disappointment or financial hardship, it seems so much more difficult to trust God's perfect plan. But, trust Him we must.

As you strive to achieve financial security for your family, remember this: The next time you find your courage tested to the limit (and it will be), lean upon God's promises. Trust His Son. Remember that God is always near and that He is your protector and your deliverer. Always.

If the Living Logos of God has the power to create and sustain the universe . . . He is more than able to sustain your marriage and your ministry, your faith and your finances, your hope and your health.

Anne Graham Lotz

Here's a recipe for handling money wisely: Take a heaping helping of common sense, add a sizeable portion of self-discipline, and mix with prayer.

Marie T. Freeman

NOW IS THE TIME

So, my son, throw yourself into this work for Christ.
2 Timothy 1:1 MSG

God's love for you is deeper and more profound than you can imagine. God's love for you is so great that He sent His only Son to this earth to die for your sins and to offer you the priceless gift of eternal life. Now, you must decide whether or not to accept God's gift. Will you ignore it or embrace it? Will you return it or neglect it? Will you accept Christ's love and build a lifelong relationship with Him, or will you turn away from Him and take a different path?

Your decision to allow Christ to reign over your heart is the pivotal decision of your life. It is a decision that you cannot ignore. It is a decision that is yours and yours alone. Accept God's gift now: allow His Son to preside over your heart, your thoughts, and your life, starting this very instant.

I can tell you, from personal experience of walking with God for over fifty years, that He is the Lover of my soul.

Vonette Bright

How important it is for us—young and old—to live as if Jesus would return any day—to set our goals, make our choices, raise our children, and conduct business with the perspective of the imminent return of our Lord.

Gloria Gaither

FORGIVING
AND FORGETTING

Real wisdom, God's wisdom, begins with a holy life and is characterized by getting along with others. It is gentle and reasonable, overflowing with mercy and blessings.

James 3:17 MSG

Do you have a tough time forgiving and forgetting? If so, welcome to the club. Most of us find it difficult to forgive the people who have hurt us. And that's too bad because life would be much simpler if we could forgive people "once and for all" and be done with it. Yet forgiveness is seldom that easy. Usually, the decision to forgive is straightforward, but the process of forgiving is more difficult. Forgiveness is a journey that requires time, perseverance, and prayer.

If you sincerely wish to forgive someone, pray for that person. And then pray for yourself by asking God to heal your heart. Don't expect forgiveness to be easy or quick, but rest assured: with God as your partner, you can forgive . . . and you will.

Forgiveness does not mean the perpetrator goes free; it means that the forgiver is free and that God will justly deal with those who have caused pain.

Cynthia Heald

If you're going to forgive somebody, why wait?

Marie T. Freeman

A HELPING HAND

The greatest among you will be your servant. For whoever exalts himself will be humbled, and whoever humbles himself will be exalted.

Matthew 23:11-12 NIV

Jesus has much to teach us about generosity. He teaches that the most esteemed men and women are not the self-congratulatory leaders of society but are, instead, the humblest of servants. If you were being graded on generosity, how would you score? Would you earn "A"s in philanthropy and humility? Hopefully so. But if your grades could stand a little improvement, this is the perfect day to begin.

Today, you may feel the urge to hoard your blessings. Don't do it. Instead, give generously to your neighbors, and do so without fanfare. Find a need and fill it . . . humbly. Lend a helping hand and share a word of kindness . . . anonymously. This is God's way.

When somebody needs a helping hand, he doesn't need it tomorrow or the next day. He needs it now, and that's exactly when you should offer to help. Good deeds, if they are really good, happen sooner rather than later.

Marie T. Freeman

HIS CALLING

But as God has distributed to each one, as the Lord has called each one, so let him walk.

1 Corinthians 7:17 NKJV

It is terribly important that you heed God's calling by discovering and developing your talents and your spiritual gifts. If you seek to make a difference—and if you seek to bear eternal fruit—you must discover your gifts and begin using them for the glory of God.

Every believer has at least one gift. In John 15:16, Jesus says, "You did not choose Me, but I chose you and appointed you that you should go and bear fruit, and that your fruit should remain, that whatever you ask the Father in My name He may give you." Have you found your special calling? If not, keep searching and keep praying until you find it. God has important work for you to do, and the time to begin that work is now.

God has given you special talents—now it's your turn to give them back to God.

Marie T. Freeman

The center of power is not to be found in summit meetings or in peace conferences. It is not in Peking or Washington or the United Nations, but rather where a child of God prays in the power of the Spirit for God's will to be done in her life, in her home, and in the world around her.

Ruth Bell Graham

FAR BEYOND ENVY

Therefore, laying aside all malice, all deceit, hypocrisy, envy, and all evil speaking, as newborn babes, desire the pure milk of the word, that you may grow thereby.

1 Peter 2:1-2 NKJV

Because we are frail, imperfect human beings, we are sometimes envious of others. But God's Word warns us that envy is sin. Thus, we must guard ourselves against the natural tendency to feel resentment and jealousy when other people experience good fortune. As believers, we have absolutely no reason to be envious of any people on earth. After all, as Christians we are already recipients of the greatest gift in all creation: God's grace. We have been promised the gift of eternal life through God's only begotten Son, and we must count that gift as our most precious possession.

So here's a simple suggestion that is guaranteed to bring you happiness: fill your heart with God's love, God's promises, and God's Son . . . and when you do so, leave no room for envy, hatred, bitterness, or regret.

What God asks, does, or requires of others is not my business; it is His.

Kay Arthur

FAITH THAT WORKS

I can already hear one of you agreeing by saying, "Sounds good. You take care of the faith department, I'll handle the works department." Not so fast. You can no more show me your works apart from your faith than I can show you my faith apart from my works. Faith and works, works and faith, fit together hand in glove.

James 2:18 MSG

Corrie ten Boom advised, "Be filled with the Holy Spirit; join a church where the members believe the Bible and know the Lord; seek the fellowship of other Christians; learn and be nourished by God's Word and His many promises. Conversion is not the end of your journey—it is only the beginning."

The work of nourishing your faith can and should be joyful work. The hours that you invest in Bible study, prayer, meditation, and worship should be times of enrichment and celebration. And, as you continue to build your life upon a foundation of faith, you will discover that the journey toward spiritual maturity lasts a lifetime. As a child of God, you are never fully "grown": instead, you can continue "growing up" every day of your life. And that's exactly what God wants you to do.

I want my life to be a faith-filled leap into his arms, knowing he will be there—not that everything will go as I want, but that he will be there and that this will be enough.

Sheila Walsh

FAITH VERSUS FEAR

Don't be afraid, because I am your God. I will make you strong and will help you; I will support you with my right hand that saves you.

Isaiah 41:10 NCV

A terrible storm rose quickly on the Sea of Galilee, and the disciples were afraid. Although they had witnessed many miracles, the disciples feared for their lives, so they turned to Jesus, and He calmed the waters and the wind.

The next time you find yourself facing a fear-provoking situation, remember that the One who calmed the wind and the waves is also your personal Savior. Then ask yourself which is stronger: your faith or your fear. The answer should be obvious. So, when the storm clouds form overhead and you find yourself being tossed on the stormy seas of life, remember this: Wherever you are, God is there, too. And, because He cares for you, you are protected.

———————

Only believe, don't fear. Our Master, Jesus, always watches over us, and no matter what the persecution, Jesus will surely overcome it.

Lottie Moon

IN FOCUS

Look straight ahead, and fix your eyes on what lies before you. Mark out a straight path for your feet; then stick to the path and stay safe. Don't get sidetracked; keep your feet from following evil.

Proverbs 4:25-27 NLT

What is your focus today? Are you willing to focus your thoughts and energies on God's blessings and upon His will for your life? Or will you turn your thoughts to other things? This day—and every day hereafter—is a chance to celebrate the life that God has given you. It's also a chance to give thanks to the One who has offered you more blessings than you can possibly count.

Today, why not focus your thoughts on the joy that is rightfully yours in Christ? Why not take time to celebrate God's glorious creation? Why not trust your hopes instead of your fears? When you do, you will think optimistically about yourself and your world . . . and you can then share your optimism with others. They'll be better for it, and so will you. But not necessarily in that order.

We are told in Scripture to focus on the Lord not on self or our circumstances. Focusing on self is sin; dwelling on our own attributes is pride; bemoaning our situation is lack of trust. None of that matters. All that matters is Christ. When we focus on him and are obedient to him, our thoughts and our actions will be what they should be.

Mary Morrison Suggs

A TERRIFIC TOMORROW

"I say this because I know what I am planning for you,"
says the Lord. "I have good plans for you, not plans to
hurt you. I will give you hope and a good future."
Jeremiah 29:11 NCV

How bright do you believe your future to be?
Well, if you're a faithful believer, God has plans for
you that are so bright that you'd better pack several
pairs of sunglasses and a lifetime supply of sunblock!

The way that you think about your future will
play a powerful role in determining how things turn
out (it's called the "self-fulfilling prophecy," and it
applies to everybody, including you). So here's another
question: Are you expecting a terrific tomorrow, or
are you dreading a terrible one? The answer to that
question will have a powerful impact on the way
tomorrow unfolds.

Today, as you live in the present and look to the
future, remember that God has an amazing plan for
you. Act—and believe—accordingly. And one more
thing: don't forget the sunblock.

Do not limit the limitless God! With Him, face the
future unafraid because you are never alone.
Mrs. Charles E. Cowman

THE THREAD OF GENEROSITY

If you have two coats, give one to the poor. If you have food, share it with those who are hungry.

Luke 3:11 NLT

The thread of generosity is woven—completely and inextricably—into the very fabric of Christ's teachings. As He sent His disciples out to heal the sick and spread God's message of salvation, Jesus offered this guiding principle: "Freely you have received, freely give" (Matthew 10:8 NIV). The principle still applies.

Lisa Whelchel spoke for Christian women everywhere when she observed, "The Lord has abundantly blessed me all of my life. I'm not trying to pay Him back for all of His wonderful gifts; I just realize that He gave them to me to give away." All of us have been blessed, and all of us are called to share those blessings without reservation. So, make this pledge and keep it: Be a cheerful, generous, courageous giver. The world needs your help, and you need the spiritual rewards that will be yours when you share your possessions, your talents, and your time.

———

A cup that is already full cannot have more added to it. In order to receive the further good to which we are entitled, we must give of that which we have.

Margaret Becker

OBEY AND BE BLESSED

If you obey my commands, you will remain in my love, just as I have obeyed my Father's commands and remain in his love.

John 15:10 NIV

God gave us His commandments for a reason: so that we might obey them and be blessed. Elisabeth Elliot advised, "Obedience to God is our job. The results of that obedience are God's." These words should serve to reminder us that obedience is imperative. But, we live in a world that presents us with countless temptations to disobey God's laws.

When we stray from God's path, we suffer. So, whenever we are confronted with sin, we have clear instructions: we must walk—or better yet run—in the opposite direction.

Don't worry about what you do not understand. Worry about what you do understand in the Bible but do not live by.

Corrie ten Boom

God asked both Noah and Joshua to do something unusual and difficult. They did it, and their obedience brought them deliverance.

Mary Morrison Suggs

ADDITIONAL RESPONSIBILITIES

The man who had received the five talents brought the other five. "Master," he said, "you entrusted me with five talents. See, I have gained five more." His master replied, "Well done, good and faithful servant! You have been faithful with a few things; I will put you in charge of many things. Come and share your master's happiness."

Matthew 25:20-21 NIV

God has promised us this: when we do our duties in small matters, He will give us additional responsibilities. Sometimes, those responsibilities come when God changes the course of our lives so that we may better serve Him. Sometimes, our rewards come in the form of temporary setbacks that lead, in turn, to greater victories. Sometimes, God rewards us by answering "no" to our prayers so that He can say "yes" to a far grander request that we, with our limited understanding, would never have thought to ask for.

If you seek to be God's servant in great matters, be faithful, be patient, and be dutiful in smaller matters. Then step back and watch as God surprises you with the spectacular creativity of His infinite wisdom and His perfect plan.

There is something incredibly comforting about knowing that the Creator is in control of your life.

Lisa Whelchel

SAFE IN GOD'S HANDS

When you pass through the waters, I will be with you;
and through the rivers, they shall not overflow you. When
you walk through the fire, you shall not be burned, nor
shall the flame scorch you. For I am the Lord your God,
The Holy One of Israel, your Savior.

Isaiah 43:2-3 NKJV

As a busy woman, you know from firsthand experience that life is not always easy. But as a recipient of God's grace, you also know that you are protected by a loving Heavenly Father.

In times of trouble, God will comfort you; in times of sorrow, He will dry your tears. When you are troubled or weak or sorrowful, God is neither distant nor disinterested. To the contrary, God is always present and always vitally engaged in the events of your life. Reach out to Him, and build your future on the rock that cannot be shaken . . . trust in God and rely upon His provisions. He can provide everything you really need . . . and far, far more.

He is within and without. His Spirit dwells within me. His armor protects me. He goes before me and is behind me.

Mary Morrison Suggs

AN ATTITUDE OF GRATITUDE

And let the peace of God rule in your hearts . . . and be ye thankful.

Colossians 3:15 KJV

For most of us, life is busy and complicated. We have countless responsibilities, some of which begin before sunrise and many of which end long after sunset. Amid the rush and crush of the daily grind, it is easy to lose sight of God and His blessings. But, when we forget to slow down and say "Thank You" to our Maker, we rob ourselves of His presence, His peace, and His joy.

Our task, as believing Christians, is to praise God many times each day. Then, with gratitude in our hearts, we can face our daily duties with the perspective and power that only He can provide.

A sense of gratitude for God's presence in our lives will help open our eyes to what he has done in the past and what he will do in the future.

Emilie Barnes

Let's thank God for allowing us to experience troubles that drive us closer to Him.

Shirley Dobson

THE BEST POLICY

The godly are directed by their honesty.

Proverbs 11:5 NLT

From the time we are children, we are taught that honesty is the best policy, but sometimes, being honest is hard. So, we convince ourselves that it's alright to tell "little white lies." But there's a problem: Little white lies tend to grow up, and when they do, they cause havoc and pain in our lives.

For Christians, the issue of honesty is not a topic for debate. Honesty is not just the best policy, it is God's policy, pure and simple. And if we are to be servants worthy of our Savior, Jesus Christ, we must avoid all lies, white or otherwise. So, if you're tempted to sow the seeds of deception (perhaps in the form of a "harmless" white lie), resist that temptation. Truth is God's way, and a lie—of whatever color—is not.

Much guilt arises in the life of the believer from practicing the chameleon life of environmental adaptation.

Beth Moore

One thing that is important for stable emotional health is honesty—with self and with others.

Joyce Meyer

IMPERFECT BEINGS, IMPERFECT FAITH

Blessed is he that trusts in the Lord.

Proverbs 16:20 NIV

Why are we humans plagued by worry? Because we are imperfect beings with imperfect faith. Even though we are Christians who have been given the assurance of salvation—even though we are Christians who have received the promise of God's love and protection—we find ourselves fretting over the countless details of everyday life. Jesus understood our concerns when He spoke the reassuring words found in Matthew 6: "Therefore I tell you, do not worry about your life . . . ."

As you consider the promises of Jesus, remember that God still sits in His heaven and you are His beloved child. Then, perhaps, you will worry a little less and trust God a little more, and that's as it should be because God is trustworthy . . . and you are protected.

Remember always that there are two things which are more utterly incompatible even than oil and water, and these two are trust and worry.

Hannah Whitall Smith

SO LAUGH!

A happy heart makes the face cheerful . . . .
Proverbs 15:13 NIV

Laughter is God's gift, and He intends that we enjoy it. Yet sometimes, because of the inevitable stresses of everyday life, laughter seems only a distant memory. As Christians we have every reason to be cheerful and to be thankful. Our blessings from God are beyond measure, starting, of course, with a gift that is ours for the asking, God's gift of salvation through Christ Jesus.

Few things in life are more absurd than the sight of a grumpy Christian. So today, as you go about your daily activities, approach life with a grin and a chuckle. After all, God created laughter for a reason . . . to use it. So laugh!

Laughter dulls the sharpest pain and flattens out the greatest stress. To share it is to give a gift of health.
Barbara Johnson

Laughter is like premium gasoline: It takes the knock out of living.

Anonymous

SHARING THE GOOD NEWS

As you go, preach this message: "The kingdom of heaven is near."

Matthew 10:7 NIV

The Good News of Jesus Christ should be shouted from the rooftops by believers the world over. But all too often, it is not. For a variety of reasons, many Christians keep their beliefs to themselves, and when they do, the world suffers because of their failure to speak up.

As believers, we are called to share the transforming message of Jesus with our families, with our neighbors, and with the world. Jesus commands us to become fishers of men. And, the time to go fishing is now. We must share the Good News of Jesus Christ today—tomorrow may indeed be too late.

Proclaim to every people, tongue and nation that God, in whom they live and move, is love.

Mary A. Thomson

There is no thrill quite as wonderful as seeing someone else come to trust Christ because I have been faithful in sharing the story of my own faith.

Vonette Bright

WISDOM IN A DONUT SHOP

*My cup runs over. Surely goodness and mercy shall follow
me all the days of my life; and I will dwell in the house of
the Lord Forever.*

Psalm 23:5-6 NKJV

Many years ago, this rhyme was posted on the
wall of a small donut shop:

As you travel through life brother,
Whatever be your goal,
Keep your eye upon the donut,
And not upon the hole.

These simple words remind us of a profound truth:
we should spend more time looking at the things we
have, not worrying about the things we don't have.

When you think about it, you've got more
blessings than you can count. So make it a habit to
thank God for the gifts He's given you, not the gifts
you wish He'd given you.

The game was to just find something about everything
to be glad about—no matter what it was. You see,
when you're hunting for the glad things, you sort of
forget the other kind.

Eleanor H. Porter

PLEASING GOD

But neither exile nor homecoming is the main thing. Cheerfully pleasing God is the main thing, and that's what we aim to do, regardless of our conditions.

2 Corinthians 5:9 MSG

When God made you, He equipped you with an array of talents and abilities that are uniquely yours. It's up to you to discover those talents and to use them, but sometimes the world will encourage you to do otherwise. At times, society will attempt to cubbyhole you, to standardize you, and to make you fit into a particular, preformed mold. Perhaps God has other plans.

Sometimes, because you're an imperfect human being, you may become so wrapped up in meeting society's expectations that you fail to focus on God's expectations. To do so is a mistake of major proportions—don't make it. Instead, seek God's guidance as you focus your energies on becoming the best "you" that you can possibly be. And, when it comes to matters of conscience, seek approval not from your peers, but from your Creator.

You will get untold flak for prioritizing God's revealed and present will for your life over man's . . . but, boy, is it worth it.

Beth Moore

COMMUNITY LIFE

Regarding life together and getting along with each other, you don't need me to tell you what to do. You're God-taught in these matters. Just love one another!

1 Thessalonians 4:9 MSG

As we travel along life's road, we build lifelong relationships with a small, dear circle of family and friends. And how best do we build and maintain these relationships? By following the Word of God. Healthy relationships are built upon honesty, compassion, responsible behavior, trust, and optimism. Healthy relationships are built upon the Golden Rule. Healthy relationships are built upon sharing and caring. All of these principles are found time and time again in God's Holy Word. When we read God's Word and follow His commandments, we enrich our own lives and the lives of those who are closest to us.

Line by line, moment by moment, special times are etched into our memories in the permanent ink of everlasting love in our relationships.

Gloria Gaither

In God's economy you will be hard-pressed to find many examples of successful "Lone Rangers."

Luci Swindoll

SHARING THE GOOD NEWS

Christ did not send me to baptize people but to preach the Good News. And he sent me to preach the Good News without using words of human wisdom so that the cross of Christ would not lose its power.

1 Corinthians 1:17 NCV

In his second letter to Timothy, Paul offers a message to believers of every generation when he writes, "God has not given us a spirit of timidity" (1:7 NASB). Paul's meaning is crystal clear: When sharing our testimonies, we, as Christians, must be courageous, forthright, and unashamed.

We live in a world that desperately needs the healing message of Christ Jesus. Every believer, each in his or her own way, bears a personal responsibility for sharing that message.

You know how Christ has touched your heart and changed your life. Now it's your turn to share the Good News with others. And remember: today is the perfect time to share your testimony because tomorrow may quite simply be too late.

Claim the joy that is yours. Pray. And know that your joy is used by God to reach others.

Kay Arthur

MISTAKES HAPPEN

Have mercy on me, O God, according to your unfailing love; according to your great compassion blot out my transgressions. Wash away all my iniquity and cleanse me from my sin.

Psalm 51:1-2 NIV

We are imperfect women living in an imperfect world; mistakes are simply part of the price we pay for being here. But, even though mistakes are an inevitable part of life's journey, repeated mistakes should not be. When we commit the inevitable blunders of life, we must correct them, learn from them, and pray to God for the wisdom not to repeat them. And then, if we are successful, our mistakes become lessons, and our lives become adventures in growth, not stagnation.

Mistakes offer the possibility for redemption and a new start in God's kingdom. No matter what you're guilty of, God can restore your innocence.

Barbara Johnson

When we focus on God, the scene changes. He's in control of our lives; nothing lies outside the realm of His redemptive grace. Even when we make mistakes, fail in relationships, or deliberately make bad choices, God can redeem us.

Penelope J. Stokes

THE GIFT OF THE SHEPHERD

*My cup runs over. Surely goodness and mercy shall follow
me all the days of my life; and I will dwell in the house of
the Lord forever.*

Psalm 23:5-6 NKJV

The Word of God is clear: Christ came in order
that we might have life abundant and life eternal.
Eternal life is the priceless possession of all who
invite Christ into their hearts, but God's abundance
is optional: He does not force it upon us.

Do you sincerely seek the riches that our Savior
offers to those who give themselves to Him? Then
follow Him completely and obey Him without
reservation. When you do, you will receive the love
and the abundance that He has promised. Seek first
the salvation that is available through a personal
relationship with Jesus Christ, and then claim His
joy, His peace, and His abundance.

Jesus intended for us to be overwhelmed by the
blessings of regular days. He said it was the reason he
had come: "I am come that they might have life, and
that they might have it more abundantly."

Gloria Gaither

You need to understand that you are being influenced
by selfish pride when you reject the gifts of God just
because they do not come in a shape that suits your
taste.

Fénelon

WHY DO BAD THINGS HAPPEN?

They won't be afraid of bad news; their hearts are steady because they trust the Lord.

Psalm 112:7 NCV

If God is good, and if He made the world, why do bad things happen? Part of that question is easy to answer, and part of it isn't. Let's get to the easy part first: Sometimes, bad things happen because people disobey God's commandments and invite sadness and heartache into God's beautiful world.

But on other occasions, bad things happen, and it's nobody's fault. So who is to blame? Sometimes, nobody is to blame. Sometimes, things just happen and we simply cannot know why. Thankfully, all our questions will be answered . . . some day. The Bible promises that in heaven we will understand all the reasons behind God's plans. But until then, we must simply trust that God is good, and that, in the end, He will make things right.

In perplexities—when we cannot tell what to do, when we cannot understand what is going on around us—let us be calmed and steadied and made patient by the thought that what is hidden from us is not hidden from Him.

Frances Ridley Havergal

PRACTICING WHAT
WE PREACH

*If the way you live isn't consistent with what you believe,
then it's wrong.*

Romans 14:23 MSG

In describing our beliefs, our actions are far better descriptors than our words. Yet far too many of us spend more energy talking about our beliefs than living by them—with predictably poor results.

As believers, we must beware: Our actions should always give credence to the changes that Christ can make in the lives of those who walk with Him.

Your beliefs shape your values, and your values shape your life. Is your life a clearly-crafted picture book of your creed? Are your actions always consistent with your beliefs? Are you willing to practice the philosophies that you preach? Hopefully so; otherwise, you'll be tormented by inconsistencies between your beliefs and your behaviors.

Those who believe they believe in God but without passion in the heart, without anguish of mind, without uncertainty, without doubt, and even at times without despair, believe only in the idea of God, and not in God himself.

Madeleine L'Engle

ALWAYS WITH US

For a child is born to us, a son is given to us. And the government will rest on his shoulders. These will be his royal titles: Wonderful Counselor, Mighty God, Everlasting Father, Prince of Peace.

Isaiah 9:6 NLT

Are you facing difficult circumstances or unwelcome changes? If so, please remember that God is far bigger than any problem you may face. So, instead of worrying about life's inevitable challenges, put your faith in the Father and His only begotten Son: "Jesus Christ is the same yesterday, today, and forever" (Hebrews 13:8 NKJV). And remember: it is precisely because your Savior does not change that you can face your challenges with courage for today and hope for tomorrow.

Life is often challenging, but as Christians, we should not be afraid. God loves us, and He will protect us. In times of hardship, He will comfort us; in times of change, He will guide our steps. When we are troubled, weak, or sorrowful, God is always with us. We must build our lives on the rock that cannot be moved . . . we must trust in God. Always.

With God, it isn't who you were that matters; it's who you are becoming.

Liz Curtis Higgs

CRITICS BEWARE

Don't pick on people, jump on their failures, criticize their faults—unless, of course, you want the same treatment. Don't condemn those who are down; that hardness can boomerang. Be easy on people; you'll find life a lot easier.

Luke 6:37 MSG

From experience, we know that it is easier to criticize than to correct. And we know that it is easier to find faults than solutions. Yet the urge to criticize others remains a powerful temptation for most of us. Our task, as obedient believers, is to break the twin habits of negative thinking and critical speech.

Negativity is highly contagious: we give it to others who, in turn, give it back to us. This cycle can be broken by positive thoughts, heartfelt prayers, and encouraging words. As thoughtful servants of a loving God, we can use the transforming power of Christ's love to break the chains of negativity. And we should.

Do not think of the faults of others but of what is good in them and faulty in yourself.

St. Teresa of Avila

Perhaps the greatest blessing that religious inheritance can bestow is an open mind, one that can listen without judging.

Kathleen Norris

A SACRIFICIAL LOVE

I am the good shepherd. The good shepherd lays down his life for the sheep.

John 10:11 NIV

How much does Christ love us? More than we, as mere mortals, can comprehend. His love is perfect and steadfast. Even though we are fallible and wayward, the Shepherd cares for us still. Even though we have fallen far short of the Father's commandments, Christ loves us with a power and depth that is beyond our understanding. The sacrifice that Jesus made upon the cross was made for each of us, and His love endures to the edge of eternity and beyond.

Christ's love changes everything. When you accept His gift of grace, you are transformed, not only for today, but also for all eternity. If you haven't already done so, accept Jesus Christ as your Savior. He's waiting patiently for you to invite Him into your heart. Please don't make Him wait a single minute longer.

We are the earthen vessels, the jars of clay, that bring the life and love of Christ to one another.

Sheila Walsh

God is my Heavenly Father. He loves me with an everlasting love. The proof of that is the Cross.

Elisabeth Elliot

GOD'S GUIDANCE

The steps of the Godly are directed by God. He delights in every detail of their lives.

Psalm 37:22 NLT

God is intensely interested in each of us, and He will guide our steps if we serve Him obediently.

When we sincerely offer heartfelt prayers to our Heavenly Father, He will give direction and meaning to our lives—but He won't force us to follow Him. To the contrary, God has given us the free will to follow His commandments . . . or not.

When we stray from God's commandments, we invite bitter consequences. But, when we follow His commandments, and when we genuinely and humbly seek His will, He touches our hearts and leads us on the path of His choosing.

Will you trust God to guide your steps? You should. When you entrust your life to Him completely and without reservation, God will give you the strength to meet any challenge, the courage to face any trial, and the wisdom to live in His righteousness and in His peace. So trust Him today and seek His guidance. When you do, your next step will be the right one.

God's leading will never be contrary to His word.

Vonette Bright

CONTENTMENT THROUGH CHRIST

The LORD gives strength to his people; the LORD blesses his people with peace.

Psalm 29:11 NIV

Everywhere we turn, or so it seems, the world promises us contentment and happiness. But the contentment that the world offers is fleeting and incomplete. Thankfully, the contentment that God offers is all encompassing and everlasting. Happiness, of course, depends less upon our circumstances than upon our thoughts. When we turn our thoughts to God, to His gifts, and to His glorious creation, we experience the joy that God intends for His children. But, when we focus on the negative aspects of life—or when we disobey God's commandments—we cause ourselves needless suffering.

Do you sincerely want to be a contented Christian? Then set your mind and your heart upon God's love and His grace. Seek first the salvation that is available through a personal relationship with Jesus Christ, and then claim the joy, the contentment, and the spiritual abundance that the Shepherd offers His sheep.

Contentment has a way of quieting insatiable desires.

Mary Hunt

ABOVE AND BEYOND
OUR CIRCUMSTANCES

We take the good days from God—why not also the bad days?

Job 2:10 MSG

All of us face difficult days. Sometimes even the most devout Christian women can become discouraged, and you are no exception. After all, you live in a world where expectations can be high and demands can be even higher.

If you find yourself enduring difficult circumstances, remember that God remains in His heaven. If you become discouraged with the direction of your day or your life, turn your thoughts and prayers to Him. He is a God of possibility, not negativity. He will guide you through your difficulties and beyond them . . . far beyond.

Worry is the senseless process of cluttering up tomorrow's opportunities with leftover problems from today.

Barbara Johnson

Worship and worry cannot live in the same heart; they are mutually exclusive.

Ruth Bell Graham

TAKING UP THE CROSS

Then He said to them all, "If anyone wants to come with Me, he must deny himself, take up his cross daily, and follow Me."

Luke 9:23 HCSB

When we have been saved by Christ, we can, if we choose, become passive Christians. We can sit back, secure in our own salvation, and let other believers spread the healing message of Jesus. But to do so is wrong. Instead, we are commanded to become disciples of the One who has saved us, and to do otherwise is a sin of omission with terrible consequences. When Jesus addressed His disciples, He warned them that each one must, "take up his cross daily and follow me" (Luke 9:23 NIV). Christ's message was clear: in order to follow Him, Christ's disciples must deny themselves and, instead, trust Him completely. Nothing has changed since then.

Do you seek to fulfill God's purpose for your life? Then follow Christ. Follow Him by picking up His cross today and every day that you live. Then, you will quickly discover that Christ's love has the power to change everything, including you.

A PRAYER

Help me, Lord, to understand what cross I am to bear this day. Give me the strength and the courage to carry that cross along the path of Your choosing so that I may be a worthy disciple of Your Son. Amen

ENCOURAGEMENT NOW!

A cheerful look brings joy to the heart, and good news gives health to the bones.

Proverbs 15:30 NIV

Barnabas, a man whose name meant "Son of Encouragement," was a leader in the early Christian church. He was known for his kindness and for his ability to encourage others. Because of Barnabas, many people were introduced to Christ. And today, as believers living in a difficult world, we must seek to imitate the "Son of Encouragement."

We imitate Barnabas when we speak kind words to our families and to our friends. We imitate Barnabas when our actions give credence to our beliefs. We imitate Barnabas when we are generous with our possessions and with our praise. We imitate Barnabas when we give hope to the hopeless and encouragement to the downtrodden.

Today, be like Barnabas: become a source of encouragement to those who cross your path. When you do so, you will quite literally change the world, one person—and one moment—at a time.

True friends will always lift you higher and challenge you to walk in a manner pleasing to our Lord.

Lisa Bevere

A PASSION FOR LIFE

Those who hope in the LORD will renew their strength. They will soar on wings like eagles; they will run and not grow weary, they will walk and not be faint.

Isaiah 40:31 NIV

Are you enthusiastic about your life and your faith? Hopefully so. But if your zest for life has waned, it is now time to redirect your efforts and recharge your spiritual batteries. And that means refocusing your priorities (by putting God first) and counting your blessings (instead of your troubles).

Nothing is more important than your wholehearted commitment to your Creator and to His only begotten Son. Your faith must never be an afterthought; it must be your ultimate priority, your ultimate possession, and your ultimate passion. When you become passionate about your faith, you'll become passionate about your life, too. And God will smile.

———————

If your heart has grown cold, it is because you have moved away from the fire of His presence.

Beth Moore

Finding your passion is the single most important ingredient for changing your world.

Nicole Johnson

STANDING UP
FOR YOUR FAITH

Be on the alert, stand firm in the faith, act like men, be strong.

1 Corinthians 16:13 NASB

Are you a woman whose faith is obvious to your family and to the world, or are you a spiritual shrinking violet? God needs more women who are willing to stand up and be counted for Him.

Genuine faith is never meant to be locked up in the heart of a believer; to the contrary, it is meant to be shared. And a woman who wishes to share God's Good News with the world should begin by sharing that message with his own family.

Through every triumph and tragedy, God will stand by your side and strengthen you . . . if you have faith in Him. Jesus taught His disciples that if they had faith, they could move mountains. You can too, and so can your family . . . if you have faith.

Talk faith. The world is better off without your uttered ignorance and morbid doubt. If you have faith in God, or man, or self, say so. If not, push back upon the shelf of silence all your thoughts, till faith shall come; no one will grieve because your lips are dumb.

Ella Wheeler Wilcox

GOOD THINKING

Be careful what you think, because your thoughts run your life.

Proverbs 4:23 NCV

Are you an upbeat believer? Are you a woman whose hopes and dreams are alive and well? Do you regularly put a smile on your face? And then, do you share that smile with family and friends? Hopefully so. After all, when you decided to allow Christ to rule over your heart, you entitled yourself to share in His promise of spiritual abundance and eternal joy. But sometimes, when pessimism and doubt invade your thoughts, you won't feel like celebrating. Why? Because thoughts are intensely powerful things.

Are you fearful, angry, bored, or worried? Are you so preoccupied with the concerns of this day that you fail to thank God for the promise of eternity? Are you confused, bitter, or pessimistic? If so, spend more time thinking about your blessings, and less time fretting about your hardships. Then, take time to thank the Giver of all things good for gifts that are, in truth, far too numerous to count.

The things we think are the things that feed our souls. If we think on pure and lovely things, we shall grow pure and lovely like them; and the converse is equally true.

Hannah Whitall Smith

THE LESSONS
OF TOUGH TIMES

I waited patiently for the LORD; he turned to me and heard my cry. He lifted me out of the slimy pit, out of the mud and mire; he set my feet on a rock and gave me a firm place to stand. He put a new song in my mouth, a hymn of praise to our God . . . .

Psalm 40:1-3 NIV

Have you experienced a recent setback? If so, look for the lesson that God is trying to teach you. Instead of complaining about life's sad state of affairs, learn what needs to be learned, change what needs to be changed, and move on. View failure as an opportunity to reassess God's will for your life. View life's inevitable disappointments as opportunities to learn more about yourself and your world.

Life can be difficult at times. And everybody makes mistakes. Your job is to make them only once.

God is able to take mistakes, when they are committed to Him, and make of them something for our good and for His glory.

Ruth Bell Graham

God helps those who help themselves, but there are times when we are quite incapable of helping ourselves. That's when God stoops down and gathers us in His arms like a mother lifts a sick child, and does for us what we cannot do for ourselves.

Ruth Bell Graham

GOD'S FORGIVENESS

If we confess our sins, he is faithful and just and will forgive us our sins and purify us from all unrighteousness.

1 John 1:9 NIV

The Bible promises you this: When you ask God for forgiveness, He will give it. No questions asked; no explanations required. God's power to forgive, like His love, is infinite. Despite your sins, God offers immediate forgiveness. And it's time to take Him up on His offer.

When it comes to forgiveness, God doesn't play favorites and neither should you. You should forgive all the people who have harmed you (not just the people who have asked for forgiveness or the ones who have made restitution). Complete forgiveness is God's way, and it should be your way, too. Anything less is not enough.

Forgiveness is actually the best revenge because it not only sets us free from the person we forgive, but it frees us to move into all that God has in store for us.

Stormie Omartian

Redeemed, how I love to proclaim it! Redeemed by the blood of the Lamb; Redeemed through His infinite mercy, His child, and forever, I am.

Fanny Crosby

HIS RIGHTFUL PLACE

You shall have no other gods before Me.

Exodus 20:3 NKJV

When Jesus was tempted by Satan, the Master's response was unambiguous. Jesus chose to worship the Lord and serve Him only. We, as followers of Christ, must follow in His footsteps by placing God first.

When we place God in a position of secondary importance, we do ourselves great harm. When we allow temptations or distractions to come between us and our Creator, we suffer. But, when we imitate Jesus and place the Lord in His rightful place—at the center of our lives—then we claim spiritual treasures that will endure forever.

To God be the glory, great things He has done; so loved He the world that He gave us His Son.

Fanny Crosby

God is everything. My focus must be on him, seeking to know him more completely and allowing him full possession of my life.

Mary Morrison Suggs

A PRAYER

Lord, You have commanded that I have no gods before You. Let me place You first in my heart, Father, and let me accept the salvation of Your Son Jesus. Then, let me encourage others to accept Your love and Your grace. Amen

THE SOURCE
OF OUR COMFORT

When doubts filled my mind, your comfort gave me renewed hope and cheer.

Psalm 94:19 NLT

In times of adversity, we are wise to remember the words of Jesus, who, when He walked on the waters, reassured His disciples, saying, "Take courage! It is I. Don't be afraid" (Matthew 14:27 NIV). Then, with Christ on His throne—and with trusted friends and loving family members at our sides—we can face our fears with courage and with faith.

Are you facing a difficult challenge? If so, remember that no problem is too big for God . . . not even yours.

———————

Friends are like a quilt with lots of different shapes, sizes, colors, and patterns of fabric. But the end result brings you warmth and comfort in a support system that makes your life richer and fuller.

Suzanne Dale Ezell

A PRAYER

Dear Lord, when I am troubled, You comfort me. When I am discouraged, You lift me up. Whatever my circumstances, Lord, I will trust Your plan for my life. And, when my family and friends are troubled, I will remind them of Your love, Your wisdom, and Your grace. Amen

MOVING ON

You have heard it said, "Love your neighbor and hate your enemy." But I tell you: Love your enemies and pray for those who persecute you, that you may be sons of your Father in heaven.

Matthew 5:43-45 NIV

Sometimes, people can be discourteous and cruel. Sometimes people can be unfair, unkind, and unappreciative. Sometimes people get angry and frustrated. So what's a Christian to do? God's answer is straightforward: forgive, forget, and move on. In Luke 6:37, Jesus instructs, "Do not judge, and you will not be judged. Do not condemn, and you will not be condemned. Forgive, and you will be forgiven" (HCSB).

Today and every day, make sure that you're quick to forgive others for their shortcomings. And when other people misbehave (as they most certainly will from time to time), don't pay too much attention. Just forgive those people as quickly as you can, and try to move on . . . as quickly as you can.

———

Some folks cause happiness wherever they go, others whenever they go.

Barbara Johnson

You can be sure you are abiding in Christ if you are able to have a Christlike love toward the people that irritate you the most.

Vonette Bright

RELYING UPON HIM

Therefore humble yourselves under the mighty hand of God, that He may exalt you at the proper time, casting all your anxiety on Him, because He cares for you.

1 Peter 5:6-7 NASB

God is a never-ending source of support and courage for those of us who call upon Him. When we are weary, He gives us strength. When we see no hope, God reminds us of His promises. When we grieve, God wipes away our tears.

Do the demands of this day threaten to overwhelm you? If so, you must rely not only upon your own resources but also upon the promises of your Father in heaven. God will hold your hand and walk with your every day of your life if you let Him. So even if your circumstances are difficult, trust the Father. His love is eternal and His goodness endures forever.

What God promises is that He always, always comes. He always shows up. He always saves. He always rescues. His timing is not ours. His methods are usually unconventional. But what we can know, what we can settle in our soul, is that He is faithful to come when we call.

Angela Thomas

Living by faith requires patience, for the one who lives by faith becomes dependent upon God.

Kay Arthur

GROWING IN CHRIST

When I was a child, I spoke and thought and reasoned as a child does. But when I grew up, I put away childish things.

1 Corinthians 13:11 NLT

The journey toward spiritual maturity lasts a lifetime. As Christians, we can and should continue to grow in the love and the knowledge of our Savior as long as we live. Norman Vincent Peale had the following advice for believers of all ages: "Ask the God who made you to keep remaking you." That advice, of course, is perfectly sound, but often ignored.

When we cease to grow, either emotionally or spiritually, we do ourselves a profound disservice. But, if we study God's Word, if we obey His commandments, and if we live in the center of His will, we will not be "stagnant" believers; we will, instead, be growing Christians . . . and that's exactly what God wants for our lives.

No matter what we are going through, no matter how long the waiting for answers, of one thing we may be sure. God is faithful. He keeps His promises. What He starts, He finishes . . . including His perfect work in us.

Gloria Gaither

RELATIONSHIPS BUILT UPON HONESTY

The honest person will live in safety, but the dishonest will be caught.

Proverbs 10:9 NCV

Lasting relationships are built upon a foundation of honesty and trust. It has been said on many occasions that honesty is the best policy. For believers, it is far more important to note that honesty is God's policy. And if we are to be servants worthy of our Savior, Jesus Christ, we must be honest and forthright in all our communications with others.

Sometimes, honesty is difficult; sometimes, honesty is painful; sometimes, honesty makes us feel uncomfortable. Despite these temporary feelings of discomfort, we must make honesty the hallmark of all our relationships; otherwise, we invite needless suffering into our own lives and into the lives of those we love.

The single most important element in any human relationship is honesty—with oneself, with God, and with others.

Catherine Marshall

Those who, to please their listeners, avoid giving a forthright declaration of the will of God become slaves of those they would please and abandon the service of God.

St. Basil the Great

TO GOD BE THE GLORY

God is against the proud, but he gives grace to the humble.

1 Peter 5:5 NCV

As Christians, we have a profound reason to be humble: We have been refashioned and saved by Jesus Christ, and that salvation came not because of our own good works but because of God's grace. Thus, we are not "self-made," we are "God-made" and "Christ-saved." How, then, can we be boastful?

Dietrich Bonhoeffer observed, "It is very easy to overestimate the importance of our own achievements in comparison with what we owe others." In other words, reality breeds humility. So, instead of puffing out your chest and saying, "Look at me!", give credit where credit is due, starting with God. And, rest assured: There is no such thing as a self-made man. All of us are made by God . . . and He deserves the glory, not us.

Without humility of heart all the other virtues by which one runs toward God seem—and are—absolutely worthless.

Angela of Foligno

Our God is so wonderfully good, and lovely, and blessed in every way that the mere fact of belonging to Him is enough for an untellable fullness of joy!

Hannah Whitall Smith

THE GREATEST OF THESE

But now abide faith, hope, love, these three; but the greatest of these is love.

1 Corinthians 13:13 NASB

The beautiful words of 1st Corinthians 13 remind us that love is God's commandment: Faith is important, of course. So, too, is hope. But, love is more important still. We are commanded (not advised, not encouraged . . . commanded!) to love one another just as Christ loved us (John 13:34). That's a tall order, but as Christians, we are obligated to follow it.

Christ showed His love for us on the cross, and we are called upon to return Christ's love by sharing it. Today, let us spread Christ's love to families, friends, and even strangers, so that through us, others might come to know Him.

———————

There are only two duties required of us—the love of God and the love of our neighbor, and the surest sign of discovering whether we observe these duties is the love of our neighbor.

St. Teresa of Avila

Prayer is the ultimate love language. It communicates in ways we can't.

Stormie Omartian

THE CORNERSTONE

Let us fix our eyes on Jesus, the author and perfecter of our faith, who for the joy set before him endured the cross, scorning its shame, and sat down at the right hand of the throne of God.

Hebrews 12:2 NIV

Is Christ the focus of your life? Are you fired with enthusiasm for Him? Are you an energized Christian who allows God's Son to reign over every aspect of your day? Make no mistake: that's exactly what God intends for you to do.

God has given you the gift of eternal life through His Son. In response to God's priceless gift, you are instructed to focus your thoughts, your prayers, and your energies upon God and His only begotten Son. To do so, you must resist the subtle yet powerful temptation to become a "spiritual dabbler." A person who dabbles in the Christian faith is unwilling to place God above all other things. Resist that temptation; make God the cornerstone and the touchstone of your life. When you do, He will give you all the strength and wisdom you need to live victoriously for Him.

––––––––

When Jesus is in our midst, He brings His limitless power along as well. But, Jesus must be in the middle, all eyes and hearts focused on Him.

Shirley Dobson

IN A HURRY?

The Lord is wonderfully good to those who wait for him and seek him. So it is good to wait quietly for salvation from the Lord.

Lamentations 3:25-26 NLT

Are you a woman in a hurry? If so, you may be in for a few disappointments. Why? Because life has a way of unfolding according to God's timetable, not yours. That's why life requires patience . . . and lots of it!

Lamentations 3:25-26 reminds us that, "The Lord is wonderfully good to those who wait for him and seek him. So it is good to wait quietly for salvation from the Lord" (NIV). But, for most of us, waiting quietly for God is difficult because we're in such a hurry for things to happen!

The next time you find your patience tested to the limit, slow down and trust God. Sometimes, we must wait patiently for Him, and that's as it should be. After all, think how patient God has been with us.

Let me encourage you to continue to wait with faith. God may not perform a miracle, but He is trustworthy to touch you and make you whole where there used to be a hole.

Lisa Whelchel

KEEPING POSSESSIONS IN PERSPECTIVE

Then Jesus said to them, "Be careful and guard against all kinds of greed. Life is not measured by how much one owns."

Luke 12:15 NCV

All too often, we focus our thoughts and energies on the accumulation of earthly treasures, leaving precious little time to accumulate the only treasures that really matter: the spiritual kind. Our material possessions have the potential to do great good or terrible harm, depending upon how we choose to use them. As believers, our instructions are clear: we must use our possessions in accordance with God's commandments, and we must be faithful stewards of the gifts He has seen fit to bestow upon us.

Today, let us honor God by placing no other gods before Him. God comes first; everything else comes next—and "everything else" most certainly includes all of our earthly possessions.

———

When we put people before possessions in our hearts, we are sowing seeds of enduring satisfaction.

Beverly LaHaye

As faithful stewards of what we have, ought we not to give earnest thought to our staggering surplus?

Elisabeth Elliot

SPIRITUAL RENEWAL

*Now we look inside, and what we see is that anyone
united with the Messiah gets a fresh start, is created new.
The old life is gone; a new life burgeons! Look at it!*
                                              2 Corinthians 5:17 MSG

Even the most inspired Christian women can,
from time to time, find themselves running on empty.
The demands of daily life can drain us of our strength
and rob us of the joy that is rightfully ours in Christ.

Are you tired or troubled? Turn your heart toward
God in prayer. Are you weak or worried? Take the
time—or, more accurately, make the time—to delve
deeply into God's Holy Word. Are you spiritually
depleted? Call upon fellow believers to support you,
and call upon Christ to renew your spirit and your
life. When you do, you'll discover that the Creator of
the universe stands always ready and always able to
create a new sense of wonderment and joy in you.

He is the God of wholeness and restoration.
                                              Stormie Omartian

A PRAYER

Lord, I am an imperfect woman. Because my faith is
limited, I may become overwhelmed by the demands
of the day. When I feel tired or discouraged, renew
my strength. When I am worried, let me turn my
thoughts and my prayers to You. Let me trust Your
promises, Dear Lord, and let me accept Your unending
love, now and forever. Amen

HIS TRANSFORMING POWER

Your old life is dead. Your new life, which is your real life—even though invisible to spectators—is with Christ in God. He is your life.

Colossians 3:3 MSG

God's hand has the power to transform your day and your life. Your task is to accept Christ's grace with a humble, thankful heart as you receive the "new life" that can be yours through Him. Righteous believers who fashion their days around Jesus see the world differently; they act differently, and they feel differently about themselves and their neighbors. Hopefully, you, too, will be such a believer.

Do you desire to improve some aspect of your life? If so, don't expect changing circumstances to miraculously transform you into the person you want to become. Transformation starts with God, and it starts in the quiet corners of a willing human heart—like yours.

———————————

God's work is not in buildings, but in transformed lives.

Ruth Bell Graham

A PRAYER

Dear Lord, let me live righteously, and let my actions be consistent with my beliefs. Let every step that I take reflect Your truth, and let me live a life that is worthy of Your Son. Amen

ACCEPTING GOD'S GIFTS

For God loved the world in this way: He gave His only Son, so that everyone who believes in Him will not perish but have eternal life.

John 3:16 HCSB

God loves you—His love for you is deeper and more profound than you can imagine. God's love for you is so great that He sent His only Son to this earth to die for your sins and to offer you the priceless gift of eternal life.

You must decide whether or not to accept God's gift. Will you ignore it or embrace it? Will you return it or neglect it? Will you invite Christ to dwell in the center of your heart, or will you relegate Him to a position of lesser importance? The decision is yours, and so are the consequences. So choose wisely . . . and choose today.

It's your heart that Jesus longs for: your will to be made His own with self on the cross forever, and Jesus alone on the throne.

Ruth Bell Graham

Acceptance says: True, this is my situation at the moment. I'll look unblinkingly at the reality of it. But, I'll also open my hands to accept willingly whatever a loving Father sends me.

Catherine Marshall

FACING LIFE'S TRIALS

Now I take limitations in stride, and with good cheer, these limitations that cut me down to size—abuse, accidents, opposition, bad breaks. I just let Christ take over! And so the weaker I get, the stronger I become.

2 Corinthians 12:10 MSG

Life is a tapestry of good days and difficult days, with good days predominating. During the good days, we are tempted to take our blessings for granted (a temptation that we must resist with all our might). But, during life's difficult days, we discover precisely what we're made of. And more importantly, we discover what our faith is made of.

Has your faith been put to the test yet? If so, then you know that with God's help, you can endure life's darker days. But if you have not yet faced the inevitable trials and tragedies of life-here-on-earth, don't worry: you will. And when your faith is put to the test, rest assured that God is perfectly willing—and always ready—to give you strength for the struggle.

Jesus, my Savior, look on me, for I am weary and oppressed; I come to cast myself on Thee: Thou art my Rest.

Charlotte Elliott

PRACTICAL CHRISTIANITY

If the way you live isn't consistent with what you believe, then it's wrong.

Romans 14:23 MSG

As Christians, we must do our best to ensure that our actions are accurate reflections of our beliefs. Our theology must be demonstrated, not only by our words but, more importantly, by our actions. In short, we should be practical believers, quick to act whenever we see an opportunity to serve God.

Are you the kind of practical Christian woman who is willing to dig in and do what needs to be done when it needs to be done? If so, congratulations: God acknowledges your service and blesses it. But if you find yourself more interested in the fine points of theology than in the needs of your neighbors, it's time to rearrange your priorities. God needs believers who are willing to roll up their sleeves and go to work for Him. Count yourself among that number. Theology is a good thing unless it interferes with God's work. And it's up to you to make certain that your theology doesn't.

Slowly I have realized that I do not have to be qualified to do what I am asked to do, that I just have to go ahead and do it, even if I can't do it as well as I think it ought to be done. This is one of the most liberating lessons of my life.

Madeleine L'Engle

BEYOND BITTERNESS

Don't insist on getting even; that's not for you to do. "I'll do the judging," says God. "I'll take care of it."

Romans 12:19 MSG

Bitterness is a spiritual sickness. It will consume your soul; it is dangerous to your emotional health. It can destroy you if you let it . . . so don't let it! If you are caught up in intense feelings of anger or resentment, you know all too well the destructive power of these emotions. How can you rid yourself of these feelings? First, you must prayerfully ask God to cleanse your heart. Then, you must learn to catch yourself whenever thoughts of bitterness or hatred begin to attack you. Your challenge is this: You must learn to resist negative thoughts before they hijack your emotions.

Matthew 5:22 teaches us that if we judge our brothers and sisters, we, too, will be subject to judgement. Let us refrain, then, from judging our neighbors. Instead, let us forgive them and love them, while leaving their judgement to a far more capable authority: the One who sits on His throne in heaven.

Bitterness is a spiritual cancer, a rapidly growing malignancy that can consume your life. Bitterness cannot be ignored but must be healed at the very core, and only Christ can heal bitterness.

Beth Moore

MID-COURSE CORRECTIONS

The prudent see danger and take refuge, but the simple keep going and suffer from it.

Proverbs 27:12 NIV

In our fast-paced world, everyday life has become an exercise in managing change. Our circumstances change; our relationships change; our bodies change. We grow older every day, as does our world. Thankfully, God does not change. He is eternal, as are the truths that are found in His Holy Word.

Are you facing one of life's inevitable "mid-course corrections"? If so, you must place your faith, your trust, and your life in the hands of the One who does not change: your Heavenly Father. He is the unmoving rock upon which you must construct this day and every day. When you do, you are secure.

We do not love each other without changing each other. We do not observe the world around us without in some way changing it, and being changed ourselves.

Madeleine L'Engle

Mistakes offer the possibility for redemption and a new start in God's kingdom. No matter what you're guilty of, God can restore your innocence.

Barbara Johnson

OUR CHILDREN, OUR HOPE

Let the little children come to Me; don't stop them, for the kingdom of God belongs to such as these.

Mark 10:14 HCSB

Every child is different, but every child is similar in this respect: he or she is a priceless gift from the Father above. And, with the Father's gift comes immense responsibilities.

Our children are our most precious resource. And, as responsible adults, we must create homes in which the future generation can grow and flourish.

Today, let us pray for our children . . . all of them. Let us pray for children here at home and for children around the world. Every child is God's child. May we, as concerned adults, behave—and pray— accordingly.

Children are not so different from kites. Children were created to fly. But, they need wind, the undergirding, and strength that comes from unconditional love, encouragement, and prayer.

Gigi Graham Tchividjian

Children are better believers than grown-ups, and better theologians than many academicians.

Madeleine L'Engle

LIVING IN CHRIST'S LOVE

And now, children, stay with Christ. Live deeply in Christ. Then we'll be ready for him when he appears, ready to receive him with open arms, with no cause for red-faced guilt or lame excuses when he arrives. Once you're convinced that he is right and righteous, you'll recognize that all who practice righteousness are God's true children.

1 John 2:28-29 MSG

Even though we are imperfect, fallible human beings, even though we have fallen far short of God's commandments, Christ loves us still. His love is perfect and steadfast; it does not waver—it does not change. Our task, as believers, is to accept Christ's love and to encourage others to do likewise.

In today's troubled world, we all need the love and the peace that is found through the Son of God. Thankfully, Christ's love has no limits; it can encircle all of us. And it's up to each of us to ensure that it does.

It has been the faith of the Son of God who loves me and gave Himself for me that has held me in the darkest valley and the hottest fires and the deepest waters.

Elisabeth Elliot

HIS POWER AND YOURS

When we were baptized, we were buried with Christ and shared his death. So, just as Christ was raised from the dead by the wonderful power of the Father, we also can live a new life.

Romans 6:4 NCV

When you invite Christ to rule over your heart, you avail yourself of His power. And make no mistake about it: You and Christ, working together, can do miraculous things. In fact, miraculous things are exactly what Christ intends for you to do, but He won't force you to do great things on His behalf. The decision to become a full-fledged participant in His power is a decision that you must make for yourself.

In John 14:12, Christ made this promise: "I tell you the truth, whoever believes in me will do the same things that I do" (NCV). So trust the Savior's promise, and expect a miracle in His name.

The amount of power you experience to live a victorious, triumphant Christian life is directly proportional to the freedom you give the Spirit to be Lord of your life!

Anne Graham Lotz

If you believe in a God who controls the big things, you have to believe in a God who controls the little things. It is we, of course, to whom things look "little" or "big."

Elisabeth Elliot

FINDING CONTENTMENT

I've learned by now to be quite content whatever my circumstances. I'm just as happy with little as with much, with much as with little. I've found the recipe for being happy whether full or hungry, hands full or hands empty.

Philippians 4:11-12 MSG

Where can we find contentment? Is it a result of wealth, power, beauty, or fame? Hardly. Genuine contentment is a gift from God to those who trust Him and follow His commandments.

Our modern world seems preoccupied with the search for happiness. We are bombarded with messages telling us that happiness depends upon the acquisition of material possessions. These messages are false. Enduring peace is not the result of our acquisitions; it is a spiritual gift from God to those who obey Him and accept His will.

If we don't find contentment in God, we will never find it anywhere else. But, if we seek Him and obey Him, we will be blessed with an inner peace that is beyond human understanding. When God dwells at the center of our lives, peace and contentment will belong to us just as surely as we belong to God.

We will never be happy until we make God the source of our fulfillment and the answer to our longings.

Stormie Omartian

DECISION-MAKING 101

An indecisive man is unstable in all his ways.

James 1:8 HCSB

From the instant you wake in the morning until the moment you nod off to sleep at night, you have the opportunity to make countless decisions: decisions about the things you do, decisions about the words you speak, and decisions about the thoughts you choose to think.

If you're facing one of life's major decisions, here are some things you can do: 1. Gather as much information as you can. 2. Don't be too impulsive. 3. Rely on the advice of trusted friends and mentors. 4. Pray for guidance. 5. Trust the quiet inner voice of your conscience. 6. When the time for action arrives, act. Procrastination is the enemy of progress; don't let it defeat you.

People who can never quite seem to make up their minds usually make themselves miserable. So when in doubt, be decisive. It's the decent way to live.

When we learn to listen to Christ's voice for the details of our daily decisions, we begin to know Him personally.

Catherine Marshall

I do not know how the Spirit of Christ performs it, but He brings us choices through which we constantly change, fresh and new, into His likeness.

Joni Eareckson Tada

DILIGENCE NOW

Do not lack diligence; be fervent in spirit; serve the Lord.

Romans 12:11 HCSB

God's Word reminds us again and again that our Creator expects us to lead disciplined lives. God doesn't reward laziness, misbehavior, or apathy. To the contrary, He expects believers to behave with dignity and discipline.

We live in a world in which leisure is glorified and indifference is often glamorized. But God has other plans. He did not create us for lives of mediocrity; He created us for far greater things. Life's greatest rewards seldom fall into our laps; to the contrary, our greatest accomplishments usually require lots of work, which is perfectly fine with God. After all, He knows that we're up to the task, and He has big plans for us; may we, as disciplined believers, always be worthy of those plans.

Real freedom means to welcome the responsibility it brings, to welcome the God-control it requires, to welcome the discipline that results, to welcome the maturity it creates.

Eugenia Price

Keep adding, keep walking, keep advancing; do not stop, do not turn back, do not turn from the straight road.

St. Augustine

SHARING WORDS OF HOPE

Let's see how inventive we can be in encouraging love and helping out, not avoiding worshipping together as some do but spurring each other on.

Hebrews 10:24-25 MSG

Hope, like other human emotions, is contagious. When we associate with hope-filled Christians, we are encouraged by their faith and optimism. But, if we spend too much time in the company of naysayers and pessimists, our attitudes, like theirs, tend to be cynical and negative.

Are you a hopeful, optimistic, encouraging believer? And do you associate with like-minded people? Hopefully so. As a faithful follower of the One from Galilee, you have every reason to be hopeful, and you have every reason to share your hopes with others. So today, look for reasons to celebrate God's endless blessings. And while you're at it, look for people who will join you in the celebration. You'll be better for their company, and they'll be better for yours.

The glory of friendship is not the outstretched hand, or the kindly smile, or the joy of companionship. It is the spiritual inspiration that comes to one when he discovers that someone else believes in him and is willing to trust him with his friendship.

Corrie ten Boom

FOR ALL ETERNITY

Truly, truly, I say to you, he who hears My word, and believes Him who sent Me, has eternal life, and does not come into judgment, but has passed out of death into life. Truly, truly, I say to you, an hour is coming and now is, when the dead will hear the voice of the Son of God, and those who hear will live.

John 5:24–25 NASB

As mere mortals, our vision for the future, like our lives here on earth, is limited. God's vision is not burdened by such limitations: His plans extend throughout all eternity. Thus, God's plans for you are not limited to the ups and downs of everyday life. Your Heavenly Father has bigger things in mind . . . much bigger things.

Let us praise the Creator for His priceless gift, and let us share the Good News with all who cross our paths. We return our Father's love by accepting His grace and by sharing His message and His love. When we do, we are blessed here on earth and throughout all eternity.

———————

Your choice to either receive or reject the Lord Jesus Christ will determine where you spend eternity.

Anne Graham Lotz

FAITH THAT MOVES MOUNTAINS

I tell you the truth, you can say to this mountain, "Go, fall into the sea." And if you have no doubts in your mind and believe that what you say will happen, God will do it for you.

Mark 11:23 NCV

Because we live in a demanding world, all of us have mountains to climb and mountains to move. Moving those mountains requires faith.

Are you a mountain mover whose faith is evident for all to see? Hopefully so. God needs more women who are willing to move mountains for His glory and for His kingdom.

God walks with you, ready and willing to strengthen you. Accept His strength today. And remember—Jesus taught His disciples that if they had faith, they could move mountains. You can too . . . so with no further ado, let the mountain-moving begin.

Not everyone possesses boundless energy or a conspicuous talent. We are not equally blessed with great intellect or physical beauty or emotional strength. But we have all been given the same ability to be faithful.

Gigi Graham Tchividjian

PLANS: YOURS AND GOD'S

People may make plans in their minds, but the Lord decides what they will do.

Proverbs 16:9 NCV

If you're like most people, you want things to happen according to your wishes and according to your timetable. But sometimes, God has other plans . . . and He always has the final word.

Are you embittered by a personal tragedy that you did not deserve and cannot understand? If so, it's time to make peace with life. It's time to forgive others, and, if necessary, to forgive yourself. It's time to accept the unchangeable past, to embrace the priceless present, and to have faith in the promise of tomorrow. It's time to trust God completely. And it's time to reclaim the peace—His peace—that can and should be yours. So, if you've encountered unfortunate circumstances that are beyond your power to control, accept those circumstances . . . and trust God. When you do, you can be comforted in the knowledge that your Creator is both loving and wise, and that He understands His plans perfectly, even when you do not.

The will of God for your life is simply that you submit yourself to Him each day and say, "Father, Your will for today is mine. Your pleasure for today is mine. Your work for today is mine. I trust You to be God. You lead me today and I will follow."

Kay Arthur

THE SEARCH
FOR SIGNIFICANCE

For everything, absolutely everything, above and below, visible and invisible, rank after rank after rank of angels— everything got started in him and finds its purpose in him.

Colossians 1:16 MSG

"What on earth does God intend for me to do with my life?" It's an easy question to ask but, for many of us, a difficult question to answer. Why? Because God's purposes aren't always clear to us. Sometimes we wander aimlessly in a wilderness of our own making. And sometimes, we struggle mightily against God in an unsuccessful attempt to find success and happiness through our own means, not His.

If you're a woman who sincerely seeks God's guidance, He will give it. But, He will make His revelations known to you in a way and in a time of His choosing, not yours, so be patient. Even on those difficult days when you are unsure which way to turn, you must never lose sight of these overriding facts: God created you for a reason; He has important work for you to do; and He's waiting patiently for you to do it. The next step is up to you.

The only Person who has ever brought sustained power and purpose into my life is the living person of God. The only words that keep making sense are His words. The only way that always stands is His way.

Angela Thomas

THE JOYS OF FRIENDSHIP

I thank my God every time I remember you.

Philippians 1:3 NIV

What is a friend? The dictionary defines the word *friend* as "a person who is attached to another by feelings of affection or personal regard." This definition is accurate, as far as it goes, but when we examine the deeper meaning of friendship, so many more descriptors come to mind: trustworthiness, loyalty, helpfulness, kindness, encouragement, humor, and cheerfulness, to mention but a few.

Today, as you consider the many blessings that God has given you, remember to thank Him for the friends He has chosen to place along your path. May you be a blessing to them, and may they richly bless you today, tomorrow, and every day that you live.

Friendship is the garden of God; what a delight to tend his planting!

Inez Bell Ley

Don't bypass the potential for meaningful friendships just because of differences. Explore them. Embrace them. Love them.

Luci Swindoll

READY. SET. GO!

Do not neglect the spiritual gift that is within you . . . .
1 Timothy 4:14 NASB

God has given you talents and opportunities that are uniquely yours. Are you willing to use your gifts in the way that God intends? And are you willing to summon the discipline that is required to develop your talents and to hone your skills? That's precisely what God wants you to do, and that's precisely what you should desire for yourself.

As you seek to expand your talents, you will undoubtedly encounter stumbling blocks along the way, such as the fear of rejection or the fear of failure. When you do, don't stumble! Just continue to refine your skills, and offer your services to God. And when the time is right, He will use you—but it's up to you to be thoroughly prepared when He does.

It is the definition of joy to be able to offer back to God the essence of what he's placed in you, be that creativity or a love of ideas or a compassionate heart or the gift of hospitality.

Paula Rinehart

Great relief and satisfaction can come from seeking God's priorities for us in each season, discerning what is "best" in the midst of many noble opportunities, and pouring our most excellent energies into those things.

Beth Moore

GREAT IS THY FAITHFULNESS

God is faithful, by whom you were called into the fellowship of His Son, Jesus Christ our Lord.

1 Corinthians 1:9 NKJV

God is faithful to us even when we are not faithful to Him. God keeps His promises to us even when we stray far from His will. He continues to love us even when we disobey His commandments. But God does not force His blessings upon us. If we are to experience His love and His grace, we must claim them for ourselves.

Are you tired, discouraged, or fearful? Be comforted: God is with you. Are you confused? Listen to the quiet voice of your Heavenly Father. Are you bitter? Talk with God and seek His guidance. Are you celebrating a great victory? Thank God and praise Him. He is the Giver of all things good. In whatever condition you find yourself, trust God and be comforted. The Father is with you now and forever.

God's faithfulness and grace make the impossible possible.

Sheila Walsh

I grew up learning to be self-reliant, but now, to grow up in Christ, I must unlearn self-reliance and learn self-distrust in light of his all-sufficiency.

Mary Morrison Suggs

INFINITE POSSIBILITIES

Is anything too hard for the LORD?

Genesis 18:14 KJV

Ours is a God of infinite possibilities. But sometimes, because of limited faith and limited understanding, we wrongly assume that God cannot or will not intervene in the affairs of mankind. Such assumptions are simply wrong.

Are you afraid to ask God to do big things in your life? Is your faith threadbare and worn? If so, it's time to abandon your doubts and reclaim your faith in God's promises. God's Holy Word makes it clear: absolutely nothing is impossible for the Lord. And since the Bible means what it says, you can be comforted in the knowledge that the Creator of the universe can do miraculous things in your own life and in the lives of your loved ones. Your challenge, as a believer, is to take God at His word, and to expect the miraculous.

We will see more and more that we are chosen not because of our ability, but because of the Lord's power, which will be demonstrated in our not being able.

Corrie ten Boom

GOD'S TIMETABLE

Humble yourselves, therefore, under God's mighty hand, that he may lift you up in due time.

1 Peter 5:6 NIV

Sometimes, the hardest thing to do is to wait. This is especially true when we're in a hurry and when we want things to happen now, if not sooner! But God's plan does not always happen in the way that we would like or at the time of our own choosing. Our task—as believing Christians who trust in a benevolent, all knowing Father—is to wait patiently for God to reveal Himself.

We human beings are, by nature, impatient. We know what we want, and we know exactly when we want it: RIGHT NOW! But, God knows better. He has created a world that unfolds according to His own timetable, not ours . . . thank goodness!

Even Jesus, clear as he was about his calling, had to get his instructions one day at a time. One time he was told to wait, another time to go.

Laurie Beth Jones

When we read of the great Biblical leaders, we see that it was not uncommon for God to ask them to wait, not just a day or two, but for years, until God was ready for them to act.

Gloria Gaither

BEYOND GUILT

There is therefore now no condemnation to those who are in Christ Jesus, who do not walk according to the flesh, but according to the Spirit.

Romans 8:1 NKJV

All of us have sinned. Sometimes our sins result from our own stubborn rebellion against God's commandments. And sometimes, we are swept up in events that are beyond our abilities to control. Under either set of circumstances, we may experience intense feelings of guilt. But God has an answer for the guilt that we feel. That answer, of course, is His forgiveness. When we confess our wrongdoings and repent from them, we are forgiven by the One who created us.

Are you troubled by feelings of guilt or regret? If so, you must repent from your misdeeds, and you must ask your Heavenly Father for His forgiveness. When you do so, He will forgive you completely and without reservation. Then, you must forgive yourself just as God has forgiven you: thoroughly and unconditionally.

If God has forgiven you, why can't you forgive yourself?

Marie T. Freeman

LOOKING BEFORE YOU LEAP

An impulsive vow is a trap; later you'll wish you could get out of it.

Proverbs 20:25 MSG

Are you, at times, just a little bit impulsive? Are you a woman who sometimes looks before she leaps? If so, God wants to have a little chat with you.

God's Word is clear: as believers, we are called to lead lives of discipline, diligence, moderation, and maturity. But the world often tempts us to behave otherwise. Everywhere we turn, or so it seems, we are faced with powerful temptations to behave in undisciplined, ungodly ways. Yet God's Word instructs us to be disciplined in our thoughts and our actions; God's Word warns us against the dangers of impulsive behavior. As believers in a just God, we should act and react accordingly.

We will always experience regret when we live for the moment and do not weigh our words and deeds before we give them life.

Lisa Bevere

Zeal without knowledge is always less useful and effective than regulated zeal, and very often is highly dangerous.

St. Bernard of Clairvaux

THE BREAD OF LIFE

Then Jesus said, "I am the bread that gives life. Whoever comes to me will never be hungry, and whoever believes in me will never be thirsty."

John 6:35 NCV

He was the Son of God, but He wore a crown of thorns. He was the Savior of mankind, yet He was put to death on a roughhewn cross made of wood. He offered His healing touch to an unsaved world, and yet the same hands that had healed the sick and raised the dead were pierced with nails.

Jesus Christ, the Son of God, was born into humble circumstances. He walked this earth, not as a ruler of men, but as the Savior of mankind. His crucifixion, a torturous punishment that was intended to end His life and His reign, instead became the pivotal event in the history of all humanity.

Jesus is the bread of life. Accept His grace. Share His love. And follow in His footsteps.

———————

Our Lord is the Bread of Life. His proportions are perfect. There never was too much or too little of anything about Him. Feed on Him for a well-balanced ration. All the vitamins and calories are there.

Vance Havner

A PROFOUND LOVE

Go after a life of love as if your life depended on it—
because it does. Give yourselves to the gifts God gives
you. Most of all, try to proclaim his truth.

1 Corinthians 14:1 MSG

As a woman, you know the profound love that you hold in your heart for your own family and friends. As a child of God, you can only imagine the infinite love that your Heavenly Father holds for you. God made you in His own image and gave you salvation through the person of His Son Jesus Christ. And now, precisely because you are a wondrous creation treasured by God, a question presents itself: What will you do in response to the Creator's love? Will you ignore it or embrace it?

When you embrace God's love, your life's purpose is forever changed. When you embrace God's love, you feel differently about yourself, your neighbors, your family, and your world. More importantly, you share God's message—and His love—with others. Your Heavenly Father—a God of infinite love and mercy—is waiting to embrace you with open arms. Accept His love today and forever.

Line by line, moment by moment, special times are etched into our memories in the permanent ink of everlasting love in our relationships.

Gloria Gaither

MENTORS THAT MATTER

The lips of the righteous feed many.

Proverbs 10:21 HCSB

Here's a simple yet effective way to strengthen your faith: Choose role models whose faith in God is strong.

When you emulate godly people, you become a more godly person yourself. That's why you should seek out mentors who, by their words and their presence, make you a better person and a better Christian.

Today, as a gift to yourself, select, from your friends and family members, a mentor whose judgement you trust. Then listen carefully to your mentor's advice and be willing to accept that advice, even if accepting it requires effort or pain, or both. Consider your mentor to be God's gift to you. Thank God for that gift, and use it for the glory of His kingdom.

It takes a wise person to give good advice, but an even wiser person to take it.

Marie T. Freeman

A PRAYER

Dear Lord, thank You for family members, for friends, and for mentors. When I am troubled, let me turn to them for help, for guidance, for comfort, and for perspective. And Father, let me be a friend and mentor to others so that my love for You may be reflected in my genuine concern for them. Amen

A PASSIONATE LIFE

Never be lacking in zeal, but keep your spiritual fervor, serving the Lord.

Romans 12:11 NIV

Are you passionate about your life, your loved ones, your work, and your faith? As a believer who has been saved by a risen Christ, you should be.

As a thoughtful Christian, you have every reason to be enthusiastic about life, but sometimes the inevitable struggles of life may cause you to feel decidedly unenthusiastic. If you feel that your enthusiasm is slowly fading away, it's time to slow down, to rest, to count your blessings, and to pray. When you feel worried or weary, you must pray fervently for God to renew your sense of wonderment and excitement. Life with God can be—and should be—a glorious adventure. Revel in it. When you do, God will most certainly smile upon your work and your life.

Exploring the desire of our hearts is not a waste of time. It is precisely the place where God is stirring.

Paula Rinehart

One can never consent to creep when one feels an impulse to soar.

Helen Keller

YOUR REAL RICHES

He said, "I came naked from my mother's womb, and I will be stripped of everything when I die. The LORD gave me everything I had, and the LORD has taken it away. Praise the name of the LORD!"

Job 1:21 NLT

Martin Luther observed, "Many things I have tried to grasp and have lost. That which I have placed in God's hands I still have." How true. Earthly riches are transitory; spiritual riches are not

In our demanding world, financial security can be a good thing, but spiritual prosperity is profoundly more important. Certainly we all need the basic necessities of life, but once we've acquired those necessities, enough is enough. Why? Because our real riches are not of this world. We are never really rich until we are rich in spirit.

I have held many things in my hands, and I have lost them all; but whatever I have placed in God's hands, that I still possess.

Corrie ten Boom

Getting things accomplished isn't nearly as important as taking time for love.

Janette Oke

REAL REPENTANCE

I preached that they should repent and turn to God and prove their repentance by their deeds.

Acts 26:20 NIV

Who among us has sinned? All of us. But the good news is this: When we do ask God's forgiveness and turn our hearts to Him, He forgives us absolutely and completely.

Genuine repentance requires more than simply offering God apologies for our misdeeds. Real repentance may start with feelings of sorrow and remorse, but it ends only when we turn away from the sin that has heretofore distanced us from our Creator. In truth, we offer our most meaningful apologies to God, not with our words, but with our actions. As long as we are still engaged in sin, we may be "repenting," but we have not fully "repented." So, if there is an aspect of your life that is distancing you from God, ask for His forgiveness, and—just as importantly—stop sinning. Now.

When true repentance comes, God will not hesitate for a moment to forgive, cast the sins in the sea of forgetfulness, and put the child on the road to restoration.

Beth Moore

A WISE MOVE

But if any of you lacks wisdom, let him ask of God, who gives to all generously and without reproach, and it will be given to him.

James 1:5 NASB

Do you seek wisdom for yourself and for your family? Of course you do. But, as a thoughtful woman living in a society that is filled with temptations and distractions, you know that it's all too easy for parents and children alike to stray far from the source of the ultimate wisdom: God's Holy Word.

When you commit yourself to daily study of God's Word—and when you live according to His commandments—you will become wise . . . in time. So, as a way of understanding God's plan for your life, study His Word and live by it. When you do, you will accumulate a storehouse of wisdom that will enrich your own life and the lives of your family members, your friends, and the world.

Knowledge can be learned, but wisdom must be earned. Wisdom is knowledge . . . lived.

Sheila Walsh

Wisdom enlarges our capacity for discovery and delight, causing wonder to grow as we grow.

Susan Lenzkes

PROMISES YOU CAN COUNT ON

God blesses the people who patiently endure testing. Afterward they will receive the crown of life that God has promised to those who love him.

James 1:12 NLT

Throughout the seasons of life, we must all endure life-altering personal losses that leave us breathless. When we do, we may be overwhelmed by fear, by doubt, or by both. Thankfully, God has promised that He will never desert us. And God keeps His promises.

Life is often challenging, but as Christians, we must trust the promises of our Heavenly Father. God loves us, and He will protect us. In times of hardship, He will comfort us; in times of sorrow, He will dry our tears. Whatever our circumstance, God is with us. His love endures, not only for today, but also for all of eternity.

Faith is a strong power, mastering any difficulty in the strength of the Lord who made heaven and earth.

Corrie ten Boom

A PRAYER

Dear Lord, when I face the inevitable disappointments of life, give me perspective and faith. When I have done my best, Father, let me live with the assurance that You are firmly in control, and that Your love endures forever. Amen

BEYOND ANXIETY

In the multitude of my anxieties within me, Your comforts delight my soul.

Psalm 94:19 NKJV

God calls us to live above and beyond anxiety. God calls us to live by faith, not by fear. He instructs us to trust Him completely, this day and forever. But sometimes, trusting God is difficult, especially when we become caught up in the incessant demands of an anxious world.

When you feel anxious—and you will—return your thoughts to God's love. Then, take your concerns to Him in prayer, and to the best of your ability, leave them there. Whatever "it" is, God is big enough to handle it. Let Him. Now.

The moment anxious thoughts invade your mind, go to the Lord in prayer. Look first to God. Then, you will see the cause of your anxiety in a whole new light.

Kay Arthur

We must lay our questions, frustrations, anxieties, and impotence at the feet of God and wait for His answer. And then receiving it, we must live by faith.

Kay Arthur

KEEPING UP APPEARANCES

We justify our actions by appearances; God examines our motives.

Proverbs 21:2 MSG

The world sees you as you appear to be; God sees you as you really are . . . He sees your heart, and He understands your intentions. The opinions of others should be relatively unimportant to you; however, God's view of you—His understanding of your actions, your thoughts, and your motivations—should be vitally important.

Few things in life are more futile than "keeping up appearances" for the sake of neighbors. What is important, of course, is pleasing your Father in heaven. You please Him when your intentions are pure and your actions are just.

God doesn't use us based on what we look like. He uses us based on the condition of our souls.

Judith Couchman

Outside appearances, things like the clothes you wear or the car you drive, are important to other people but totally unimportant to God. Trust God.

Marie T. Freeman

THE DIRECTION
OF YOUR THOUGHTS

*My cup runs over. Surely goodness and mercy shall follow
me all the days of my life; and I will dwell in the house of
the Lord Forever.*

Psalm 23:5-6 NKJV

God has given you free will, including the ability
to influence the direction and the tone of your
thoughts. And, here's how God wants you to direct
those thoughts: "Finally brothers, whatever is true,
whatever is honorable, whatever is just, whatever is
pure, whatever is lovely, whatever is commendable—
if there is any moral excellence and if there is any
praise—dwell on these things" (Philippians 4:8
HCSB).

The quality of your attitude will help determine
the quality of your life, so you must guard your thoughts
accordingly. If you make up your mind to approach
life with a healthy mixture of realism and optimism,
you'll be rewarded. But, if you allow yourself to fall
into the unfortunate habit of negative thinking, you
will doom yourself to unhappiness or mediocrity, or
worse. So, the next time you find yourself dwelling
upon the negative aspects of your life, refocus your
attention on things positive. That's the wise way to
direct your thoughts.

I became aware of one very important concept I had
missed before: my attitude—not my circumstances—
was what was making me unhappy.

Vonette Bright

COURAGE DURING TIMES OF CHANGE

Therefore do not worry about tomorrow, for tomorrow will worry about itself. Each day has enough trouble of its own.

Matthew 6:34 NIV

Are you anxious about situations that you cannot control? Take your anxieties to God. Are you troubled about changes that threaten to disrupt your life? Take your troubles to Him. Does your corner of the world seem to be trembling beneath your feet? Seek protection from the One who cannot be moved.

The same God who created the universe will protect you if you ask Him . . . so ask Him . . . and then serve Him with willing hands and a trusting heart. And rest assured that the world may change moment by moment, but God's love endures—unfathomable and unchanging—forever.

If God has you in the palm of his hand and your real life is secure in him, then you can venture forth—into the places and relationships, the challenges, the very heart of the storm—and you will be safe there.

Paula Rinehart

God knows that the strength that comes from wrestling with our fear will give us wings to fly.

Paula Rinehart

CHOOSING WISELY

But the wisdom that is from above is first pure, then peaceable, gentle, willing to yield, full of mercy and good fruits, without partiality and without hypocrisy.

James 3:17 NKJV

Because we are creatures of free will, we make choices—lots of them. When we make choices that are pleasing to our Heavenly Father, we are blessed. When we make choices that cause us to walk in the footsteps of God's Son, we enjoy the abundance that Christ has promised to those who follow Him. But when we make choices that are displeasing to God, we sow seeds that have the potential to bring forth a bitter harvest.

Today, as you encounter the challenges of everyday living, you will make hundreds of choices. Choose wisely. Make your thoughts and your actions pleasing to God. And remember: every choice that is displeasing to Him is the wrong choice—no exceptions.

Faith is not a feeling; it is action. It is a willed choice.

Elisabeth Elliot

No matter how many books you read, no matter how many schools you attend, you're never really wise until you start making wise choices.

Marie T. Freeman

HIS INFINITE LOVE

For I am convinced that neither death, nor life, nor angels, nor principalities, nor things present, nor things to come, nor powers, nor height, nor depth, nor any other created thing, will be able to separate us from the love of God, which is in Christ Jesus our Lord.

Romans 8:38-39 NASB

Christ's love for you is personal. He loves you so much that He gave His life in order that you might spend all eternity with Him. Christ loves you individually and intimately; His is a love unbounded by time or circumstance. Are you willing to experience an intimate relationship with Him? Your Savior is waiting patiently; don't make Him wait a single minute longer. Embrace His love today.

I am Thine, O Lord; I have heard Thy voice, and it told Thy love to me. But I long to rise in the arms of faith and be closer drawn to Thee.

Fanny Crosby

God is every moment totally aware of each one of us. Totally aware in intense concentration and love. No one passes through any area of life, happy or tragic, without the attention of God with him.

Eugenia Price

GOD, WORSHIP, AND MARRIAGE

We love Him because He first loved us.

1 John 4:19 NKJV

If you're married, you already know that it takes cooperation and commitment to build a life together. But something else is necessary as well: you and your husband should worship together. When the two of you sincerely embrace God's love, you will feel differently about yourself, your marriage, your family, and your world. When you and your husband embrace God's love together, your marriage will be transformed. And, when the two of you accept the Father's grace and share His love, you will be blessed here on earth and throughout eternity.

So, if you genuinely seek to build a marriage that will stand the test of time, make God the centerpiece. When you do, your love will endure for a lifetime and beyond.

———————

Those who abandon ship the first time it enters a storm miss the calm beyond. And the rougher the storms weathered together, the deeper and stronger real love grows.

Ruth Bell Graham

All the wealth of the world cannot be compared with the happiness of living together happily united.

Margaret of Youville

THE BATTLE IS WON

Cast your burden upon the Lord and He will sustain you:
He will never allow the righteous to be shaken.

Psalm 55:22 NASB

Christians have every reason to live courageously. After all, the ultimate battle has already been won on the cross at Calvary. But even dedicated followers of Christ may find their courage tested by the inevitable disappointments and fears that visit the lives of believers and non-believers alike.

When you find yourself worried about the challenges of today or the uncertainties of tomorrow, you must ask yourself whether or not you are ready to place your concerns and your life in God's all-powerful, all-knowing, all-loving hands. If the answer to that question is yes—as it should be—then you can draw courage today from the source of strength that never fails: your Heavenly Father.

What is courage? It is the ability to be strong in trust, in conviction, in obedience. To be courageous is to step out in faith—to trust and obey, no matter what.

Kay Arthur

A PRAYER

Lord, sometimes, this world can be a fearful place, but You have promised me that You are with me always. Today, Lord, I will live courageously as I place my trust in Your everlasting power and my faith in Your everlasting love. Amen

SOLVING LIFE'S RIDDLES

If you need wisdom—if you want to know what God wants you to do—ask him, and he will gladly tell you. He will not resent your asking.

James 1:5 NLT

Life presents each of us with countless questions, conundrums, doubts, and problems. Thankfully, the riddles of everyday living are not too difficult to solve if we look for answers in the right places. When we have questions, we should consult God's Word, we should seek the guidance of the Holy Spirit, and we should trust the counsel of God-fearing friends and family members.

Are you facing a difficult decision? Take your concerns to God and avail yourself of the messages and mentors that He has placed along your path. When you do, God will speak to you in His own way and in His own time, and when He does, you can most certainly trust the answers that He gives.

The location of your affections will drive the direction of your decisions.

Lisa Bevere

When considering the size of your problems, there are two categories that you should never worry about: the problems that are small enough for you to handle, and the ones that aren't too big for God to handle.

Marie T. Freeman

ENTHUSIASTIC DISCIPLESHIP

Do your work with enthusiasm. Work as if you were serving the Lord, not as if you were serving only men and women.

Ephesians 6:7 NCV

With whom will you choose to walk today? Will you walk with shortsighted people who honor the ways of the world, or will you walk with the Son of God? Jesus walks with you. Are you walking with Him? Hopefully, you will choose to walk with Him today and every day of your life. Jesus has called upon believers of every generation (and that includes you) to follow in His footsteps. And God's Word promises that when you follow in Christ's footsteps, you will learn how to live freely and lightly (Matthew 11:28-30).

Jesus doesn't want you to be a run-of-the-mill, follow-the-crowd kind of person. Jesus wants you to be a "new creation" through Him. And that's exactly what you should want for yourself, too. Jesus deserves your extreme enthusiasm; the world deserves it; and you deserve the experience of sharing it.

When Jesus put the little child in the midst of His disciples, He did not tell the little child to become like His disciples; He told the disciples to become like the little child.

Ruth Bell Graham

DEFEATING DISCOURAGEMENT

The Lord is the One who will go before you. He will be with you; He will not leave you or forsake you. Do not be afraid or discouraged.

Deuteronomy 31:8 HCSB

When we fail to meet the expectations of others (or, for that matter, the expectations that we have set for ourselves), we may be tempted to abandon hope. Thankfully, on those cloudy days when our strength is sapped and our faith is shaken, there exists a source from which we can draw courage and wisdom. That source is God.

When we seek to form a more intimate and dynamic relationship with our Creator, He renews our spirits and restores our souls. God's promise is made clear in Isaiah 40:31: "But those who wait on the Lord shall renew their strength; They shall mount up with wings like eagles, They shall run and not be weary, They shall walk and not faint" (NKJV). And upon this promise we can—and should—depend.

Working in the vineyard, working all the day, never be discouraged, only watch and pray.

Fanny Crosby

LIFE ETERNAL

Because I live, you will live also.

John 14:19 NASB

How marvelous it is that God became a man and walked among us. Had He not chosen to do so, we might feel removed from a distant Creator. But ours is not a distant God. Ours is a God who understands— far better than we ever could—the essence of what it means to be human.

God understands our hopes, our fears, and our temptations. He understands what it means to be angry and what it costs to forgive. He knows the heart, the conscience, and the soul of every person who has ever lived, including you. And God has a plan of salvation that is intended for you. Accept it. Accept God's gift through the person of His Son Christ Jesus, and then rest assured: God walked among us so that you might have eternal life; amazing though it may seem, He did it for you.

If you are a believer, your judgment will not determine your eternal destiny. Christ's finished work on Calvary was applied to you the moment you accepted Christ as Savior.

Beth Moore

EXCELLENCE, NOT EXCUSES

And now, children, stay with Christ. Live deeply in Christ. Then we'll be ready for him when he appears, ready to receive him with open arms, with no cause for red-faced guilt or lame excuses when he arrives.

1 John 2:28-29 MSG

We live in a world where excuses are everywhere. And it's precisely because excuses are so numerous that they are also so ineffective. When we hear the words, "I'm sorry but . . . ," most of us know exactly what is to follow: the excuse. The dog ate the homework. Traffic was terrible. It's the company's fault. The boss is to blame. The equipment is broken. We're out of that. And so forth, and so on.

Because we humans are such creative excuse-makers, all of the really good excuses have already been taken. In fact, the high-quality excuses have been used, re-used, over-used, and ab-used. That's why excuses don't work—we've heard them all before.

So, if you're wasting your time trying to concoct a new and improved excuse, don't bother. It's impossible. A far better strategy is this: do the work. Now. And let your excellent work speak loudly and convincingly for itself.

Making up a string of excuses is usually harder than doing the work.

Marie T. Freeman

FEARING GOD

The fear of the Lord is the beginning of knowledge, but fools despise wisdom and discipline.

Proverbs 1:7 NIV

Are you a woman who possesses a healthy, fearful respect for God's power? Hopefully so. After all, God's Word teaches that the fear of the Lord is the beginning of knowledge (Proverbs 1:7).

When we fear the Creator—and when we honor Him by obeying His commandments—we receive God's approval and His blessings. But, when we ignore Him or disobey His commandments, we invite disastrous consequences. God's hand shapes the universe, and it shapes our lives. As believers, we must cultivate a sincere respect for God's awesome power. The fear of the Lord is, indeed, the beginning of knowledge. So today, as you face the realities of everyday life, remember this: until you acquire a healthy, respectful fear of God's power, your education is incomplete, and so is your faith.

Spiritual worship comes from our very core and is fueled by an awesome reverence and desire for God.

Beth Moore

A WALK WITH GOD

I've laid down a pattern for you. What I've done, you do.

John 13:15 MSG

Each day, we are confronted with countless opportunities to serve God and to follow in the footsteps of His Son. When we do, our Heavenly Father guides our steps and blesses our endeavors. As citizens of a fast-changing world, we face challenges that sometimes leave us feeling overworked, over-committed, and overwhelmed. But God has different plans for us. He intends that we slow down long enough to praise Him and to glorify His Son. When we do, He lifts our spirits and enriches our lives.

Today provides a glorious opportunity to place yourself in the service of the One who is the Giver of all blessings. May you seek His will, may you trust His word, and may you walk in the footsteps of His Son.

Will you, with a glad and eager surrender, hand yourself and all that concerns you over into his hands? If you will do this, your soul will begin to know something of the joy of union with Christ.

Hannah Whitall Smith

Waiting on God is the same as walking with God toward exciting new rooms of potential and service.

Susan Lenzkes

FRIENDS AND FAMILY

As iron sharpens iron, a friend sharpens a friend.
Proverbs 27:17 NLT

A loving family is a treasure from God; so is a trustworthy friend. If you are a member of a close knit, supportive family, offer a word of thanks to your Creator. And if you have a close circle of trustworthy friends, consider yourself richly blessed.

Today, let us praise God for our family and for our friends. God has placed these people along our paths. Let us love them and care for them. And, let us give thanks to the Father for all the people who enrich our lives. These people are, in a very real sense, gifts from God; we should treat them as such.

The best times in life are made a thousand times better when shared with a dear friend.
Luci Swindoll

Giving unselfishly to our own families tests the true heart of a servant of God.
Mother Teresa

A PRAYER

Heavenly Father, thank You for my friends and family. Let me be a trustworthy friend to all, and let my love for You be reflected in my genuine love for them. Amen

THE SHEPHERD'S CARE

For Your righteousness, O God, reaches to the heavens,
You who have done great things.

Psalm 71:19 NASB

It's a promise that is made over and over again in the Bible: Whatever "it" is, God can handle it.

Life isn't always easy. Far from it! Sometimes, life can be very, very difficult. But even then, even during our darkest moments, we're protected by a loving Heavenly Father. When we're worried, God can reassure us; when we're sad, God can comfort us. When our hearts are broken, God is not just near, He is here. So we must lift our thoughts and prayers to Him. When we do, He will answer our prayers. Why? Because He is our shepherd, and He has promised to protect us now and forever.

When considering the size of your problems, there are two categories that you should never worry about: the problems that are small enough for you to handle, and the ones that aren't too big for God to handle.

Marie T. Freeman

Are you serious about wanting God's guidance to become a personal reality in your life? The first step is to tell God that you know you can't manage your own life; that you need his help.

Catherine Marshall

THE GIFT OF GRACE

For it is by grace you have been saved, through faith—
and this not from yourselves, it is the gift of God—not by
works, so that no one can boast.

Ephesians 2:8-9 NIV

God has given us so many gifts, but none can compare with the gift of salvation. We have not earned our salvation; it is a gift from God. When we accept Christ into our hearts, we are saved by His grace.

God's grace is the ultimate gift, and we owe to Him the ultimate in thanksgiving. Let us praise the Creator for His priceless gift, and let us share the Good News with all who cross our paths. We return our Father's love by accepting His grace and by sharing His message and His love. When we do, we are eternally blessed . . . and the Father smiles.

There is no secret that can separate you from God's love; there is no secret that can separate you from His blessings; there is no secret that is worth keeping from His grace.

Serita Ann Jakes

It's clear to me that our gossamer-thin lives are held together by the glue of God's grace.

Sheila Walsh

SENSING HIS PRESENCE

*Where can I go from your Spirit? Where can I flee from
your presence? If I go up to the heavens, you are there;
if I make my bed in the depths, you are there. If I rise on
the wings of the dawn, if I settle on the far side of the sea,
even there your hand will guide me, your right hand will
hold me fast.*

Psalm 139:7-10 NIV

If God is everywhere, why does He sometimes
seem so far away? The answer to that question, of
course, has nothing to do with God and everything
to do with us.

When we begin each day on our knees, in praise
and worship to Him, God often seems very near
indeed. But, if we ignore God's presence or—worse
yet—rebel against it altogether, the world in which
we live becomes a spiritual wasteland.

Today, and every day hereafter, thank God
and praise Him. He is the Giver of all things good.
Wherever you are, whether you are happy or sad,
victorious or vanquished, celebrate God's presence.
And be comforted. For He is here.

The tender eyes of God perpetually see us. He has
never stopped noticing.

Angela Thomas

It is God to whom and with whom we travel, and
while He is the End of our journey, He is also at every
stopping place.

Elisabeth Elliot

A ONE-OF-A-KIND TREASURE

Every word of God is flawless; he is a shield to those who take refuge in him.

Proverbs 30:5 NIV

God's Word is a roadmap for life here on earth and for life eternal. As Christians, we are called upon to study God's Holy Word, to trust its promises, to follow its commandments, and to share its Good News with the world.

As believers, we must study the Bible and meditate upon its meaning for our lives. Otherwise, we deprive ourselves of a priceless gift from our Creator. God's Holy Word is, indeed, a transforming, life-changing, one-of-a-kind treasure. And, a passing acquaintance with the Good Book is insufficient for Christians who seek to obey God's Word and to understand His will. After all, neither man nor woman should live by bread alone . . .

Weave the unveiling fabric of God's word through your heart and mind. It will hold strong, even if the rest of life unravels.

Gigi Graham Tchividjian

Only through routine, regular exposure to God's Word can you and I draw out the nutrition needed to grow a heart of faith.

Elizabeth George

ABUNDANT PEACE

And the peace of God, which surpasses all comprehension,
will guard your hearts and your minds in Christ Jesus.

Philippians 4:7 NASB

Are you the kind of woman who accepts God's spiritual abundance without reservation? If so, you are availing yourself of the peace and the joy that He has promised. Do you sincerely seek the riches that our Savior offers to those who give themselves to Him? Then follow Him. When you do, you will receive the love and the abundance that Jesus offers to those who follow Him.

Seek first the salvation that is available through a personal, passionate relationship with Christ, and then claim the joy, the peace, and the spiritual abundance that the Shepherd offers His sheep.

———————

God has promised us abundance, peace, and eternal life. These treasures are ours for the asking; all we must do is claim them. One of the great mysteries of life is why on earth do so many of us wait so very long to lay claim to God's gifts?

Marie T. Freeman

Peace comes only when we acknowledge that human effort cannot sustain righteousness any more than it could create it.

Susan Lenzkes

A TIME TO REST

Come to me, all you who are weary and burdened, and I will give you rest. Take my yoke upon you and learn from me, for I am gentle and humble in heart, and you will find rest for your souls. For my yoke is easy and my burden is light.

Matthew 11:28-30 NIV

Sometimes, the struggles of life can drain us of our strength. When we find ourselves tired, discouraged, or worse, there is a source from which we can draw the power needed to recharge our spiritual batteries. That source, of course, is God.

God expects us to work hard, but He also intends for us to rest. When we fail to take the rest that we need, we do a disservice to ourselves and to our families.

Is your spiritual battery running low? Is your energy on the wane? Are your emotions frayed? If so, it's time to turn your thoughts and your prayers to God. And when you're finished, it's time to rest.

If we stay with the Lord, enduring to the end of His great plan for us, we will enjoy the rest that results from living in the kingdom of God.

Serita Ann Jakes

JOY AND THE CHRISTIAN LIFE

Light shines on those who do right; joy belongs to those who are honest. Rejoice in the Lord, you who do right. Praise his holy name.

Psalm 97:11-12 NCV

God's Word makes it clear: He intends that His joy should become our joy. The Lord intends that believers should share His love with His joy in their hearts. Yet sometimes, amid the inevitable hustle and bustle of life-here-on-earth, we can forfeit—albeit temporarily—God's joy as we wrestle with the challenges of daily living.

Joni Eareckson Tada spoke for Christian women of every generation when she observed, "I wanted the deepest part of me to vibrate with that ancient yet familiar longing, that desire for something that would fill and overflow my soul."

If, today, your heart is heavy, open the door of your soul to Christ. He will give you peace and joy. And if you already have the joy of Christ in your heart, share it freely, just as Christ freely shared His joy with you.

As I contemplate all the sacrifices required in order to live a life that is totally focused on Jesus Christ and His eternal kingdom, the joy seeps out of my heart onto my face in a smile of deep satisfaction.

Anne Graham Lotz

THE WORLD . . . AND YOU

Don't copy the behavior and customs of this world, but let God transform you into a new person by changing the way you think.

Romans 12:2 NLT

We live in the world, but we must not worship it. Our duty is to place God first and everything else second. But because we are fallible beings with imperfect faith, placing God in His rightful place is often difficult. In fact, at every turn, or so it seems, we are tempted to do otherwise.

The 21st-century world is a noisy, distracting place filled with countless opportunities to stray from God's will. The world seems to cry, "Worship me with your time, your money, your energy, and your thoughts!" But God commands otherwise: He commands us to worship Him and Him alone; everything else must be secondary.

I have a divided heart, trying to love God and the world at the same time. God says, "You can't love me as you should if you love this world too."

Mary Morrison Suggs

As we have by faith said no to sin, so we should by faith say yes to God and set our minds on things above, where Christ is seated in the heavenlies.

Vonette Bright

THE TREASURE HUNT

For where your treasure is, there your heart will be also.
Luke 12:34 NKJV

All of humanity is engaged in a colossal, worldwide treasure hunt. Some people seek treasure from earthly sources, treasures such as material wealth or public acclaim; others seek God's treasures by making Him the cornerstone of their lives.

What kind of treasure hunter are you? Are you so caught up in the demands of everyday living that you sometimes allow the search for worldly treasures to become your primary focus? If so, it's time to think long and hard about what you value, and why. All the items on your daily to-do list are not created equal. That's why you must put first things first by placing God in His rightful place: first place. The world's treasures are difficult to find and difficult to keep; God's treasures are ever-present and everlasting. Which treasures, then, will you claim as your own?

It's sobering to contemplate how much time, effort, sacrifice, compromise, and attention we give to acquiring and increasing our supply of something that is totally insignificant in eternity.

Anne Graham Lotz

AT PEACE
WITH YOUR PURPOSE

But now in Christ Jesus you who once were far off have been brought near by the blood of Christ. For He Himself is our peace.

Ephesians 2:13–14 NKJV

Are you at peace with the direction of your life? If you're a Christian, you should be. Perhaps you seek a new direction or a sense of renewed purpose, but those feelings should never rob you of the genuine peace that can and should be yours through a personal relationship with Jesus.

Have you found the lasting peace that can be yours through Jesus, or are you still rushing after the illusion of "peace and happiness" that our world promises but cannot deliver? Today, as a gift to yourself, to your family, and to your friends, claim the inner peace that is your spiritual birthright: the peace of Jesus Christ.

Peace is full confidence that God is Who He says He is and that He will keep every promise in His Word.

Dorothy Harrison Pentecost

You're the only one who can do what you do.

Lois Evans

CONSTANT PRAISE

Through Him then, let us continually offer up a sacrifice of praise to God, that is, the fruit of lips that give thanks to His name.

Hebrews 13:15 NASB

The Bible makes it clear: it pays to praise God. But sometimes, we allow ourselves to become so preoccupied with the demands of daily life that we forget to say "Thank You" to the Giver of all good gifts.

Worship and praise should be a part of everything we do. Otherwise, we quickly lose perspective as we fall prey to the demands of the moment.

Do you sincerely desire to be a worthy servant of the One who has given you eternal love and eternal life? Then praise Him for who He is and for what He has done for you. Praise Him all day long, every day, for as long as you live . . . and then for all eternity.

———

God is worthy of our praise and is pleased when we come before Him with thanksgiving.

Shirley Dobson

A PRAYER

Heavenly Father, I come to You today with hope in my heart and praise on my lips. I place my trust in You, Dear Lord, knowing that with You as my Protector, I have nothing to fear. I thank You, Lord, for Your grace, for Your love, and for Your Son. Amen

HONORING GOD

Honor GOD with everything you own; give him the first and the best. Your barns will burst, your wine vats will brim over.

Proverbs 3:9-10 MSG

Whom will you choose to honor today? If you honor God and place Him at the center of your life, every day is a cause for celebration. But if you fail to honor your Heavenly Father, you're asking for trouble, and lots of it.

At times, your life is probably hectic, demanding, and complicated. When the demands of life leave you rushing from place to place with scarcely a moment to spare, you may fail to pause and thank your Creator for the blessings He has bestowed upon you. But that's a big mistake. So honor God for who He is and for what He has done for you. And don't just honor Him on Sunday morning. Praise Him all day long, every day, for as long as you live . . . and then for all eternity.

The Holy Spirit testifies of Jesus. So when you are filled with the Holy Spirit you speak about our Lord and really live to His honor.

Corrie ten Boom

This is my story, this is my song, praising my Savior all the day long; this is my story, this is my song, praising my Savior all the day long.

Fanny Crosby

ENDURING DIFFICULT DAYS

I have heard your prayer, I have seen your tears; surely I will heal you.

2 Kings 20:5 NKJV

From time to time, all of us must endure discouragement. And, we sometimes experience life-changing personal losses that leave us reeling. When we do, God stands ready to protect us. When we are troubled, we must call upon God, and, in His own time and according to His own plan, He will heal us.

Are you anxious? Take those anxieties to God. Are you troubled? Take your troubles to Him. Does your world seem to be trembling beneath your feet? Seek protection from the One who cannot be moved. The same God who created the universe will protect you if you ask Him . . . so ask Him.

Often, in the midst of great problems, we stop short of the real blessing God has for us, which is a fresh vision of who He is.

Anne Graham Lotz

When life is difficult, God wants us to have a faith that trusts and waits.

Kay Arthur

GOD HEALS US

I have heard your prayer, I have seen your tears; surely I will heal you.

2 Kings 20:5 NKJV

Women of every generation have experienced adversity, and this generation is no different. But, today's women face challenges that previous generations could have scarcely imagined. Thankfully, although the world continues to change, God's love remains constant. And, He remains ready to comfort us and strengthen us whenever we turn to Him. Psalm 147 promises, "He heals the brokenhearted, and binds their wounds" (v. 3). When we are troubled, we must call upon God, and, in His own time and according to His own plan, He will heal us.

———

God's peace is like a river, not a pond. In other words, a sense of health and well-being, both of which are expressions of the Hebrew shalom, can permeate our homes even when we're in white-water rapids.

Beth Moore

Jesus Christ is the One by Whom, for Whom, through Whom everything was made. Therefore, He knows what's wrong in your life and how to fix it.

Anne Graham Lotz

LIVING IN
AN ANXIOUS WORLD

Cast all your anxiety on him because he cares for you.
1 Peter 5:7 NIV

We live in a world that often breeds anxiety and fear. When we come face-to-face with tough times, we may fall prey to discouragement, doubt, or depression. But our Father in heaven has other plans. God has promised that we may lead lives of abundance, not anxiety. In fact, His Word instructs us to "be anxious for nothing" (Philippians 4:6). But how can we put our fears to rest? By taking those fears to God and leaving them there.

As you face the challenges of daily life, you may find yourself becoming anxious, troubled, discouraged, or fearful. If so, turn every one of your concerns over to your Heavenly Father. The same God who created the universe will comfort you if you ask Him . . . so ask Him and trust Him. And then watch in amazement as your anxieties melt into the warmth of His loving hands.

———————

When you are anxious, it means that you aren't trusting God completely; it means that you aren't trusting God to take care your needs.

Stormie Omartian

ULTIMATE ACCOUNTABILITY

Walk in a manner worthy of the God who calls you into His own kingdom and glory.

1 Thessalonians 2:12 NASB

For most of us, it is a daunting thought: one day, perhaps soon, we'll come face-to-face with our Heavenly Father, and we'll be called to account for our actions here on earth. Our personal histories will certainly not be surprising to God; He already knows everything about us. But the full scope of our activities may be surprising to us: some of us will be pleasantly surprised; others will not be.

Today, do whatever you can to ensure that your thoughts and your deeds are pleasing to your Creator. Because you will, at some point in the future, be called to account for your actions. And the future may be sooner than you think.

There may be no trumpet sound or loud applause when we make a right decision, just a calm sense of resolution and peace.

Gloria Gaither

Be eager for more frequent gatherings for thanksgiving to God and for his glory. For when you meet frequently the forces of Satan are annulled and his destructive power is canceled in the concord of our faith.

Ignatius of Antioch

THE FUTILITY OF BLAME

Walking down the street, Jesus saw a man blind from birth. His disciples asked, "Rabbi, who sinned: this man or his parents, causing him to be born blind?" Jesus said, "You're asking the wrong question. You're looking for someone to blame. There is no such cause-effect here. Look instead for what God can do."

John 9:1-3 MSG

To blame others for our own problems is the height of futility. Yet blaming others is a favorite human pastime. Why? Because blaming is much easier than fixing, and criticizing others is so much easier than improving ourselves. So instead of solving our problems legitimately (by doing the work required to solve them), we are inclined to fret, to blame, and to criticize, while doing precious little else. When we do, our problems, quite predictably, remain unsolved.

Have you acquired the bad habit of blaming others for problems that you could or should solve yourself? If so, you are not only disobeying God's Word; you are also wasting your own precious time. So, instead of looking for someone to blame, look for something to fix, and then get busy fixing it. And as you consider your own situation, remember this: God has a way of helping those who help themselves, but He doesn't spend much time helping those who don't.

You'll never win the blame game, so why even bother to play?

Marie T. Freeman

ABUNDANT LIVING

I came so they can have real and eternal life, more and better life than they ever dreamed of.

John 10:10 MSG

The familiar words of John 10:10 should serve as a daily reminder: Christ came to this earth so that we might experience His abundance, His love, and His gift of eternal life. But as every woman knows, some days are so busy and so hurried that abundance seems a distant promise. It is not. Every day, we can claim the spiritual abundance that God promises for our lives . . . and we should.

Christ is the ultimate Savior of mankind and the personal Savior of those who believe in Him. As His servants, we should place Him at the very center of our lives. And, every day that God gives us breath, we should share Christ's love and His abundance with a world that needs both.

If you want purpose and meaning and satisfaction and fulfillment and peace and hope and joy and abundant life that lasts forever, look to Jesus.

Anne Graham Lotz

COMMISSIONED TO WITNESS

Therefore go and make disciples of all nations, baptizing them in the name of the Father and of the Son and of the Holy Spirit, and teaching them to obey everything I have commanded you. And surely I am with you always, to the very end of the age.

Matthew 28:19-20 NIV

After His resurrection, Jesus addressed His disciples. As recorded in the 28th chapter of Matthew, Christ instructed His followers to share His message with the world. This "Great Commission" applies to Christians of every generation, including our own.

As believers, we are called to share the Good News of Jesus with our families, with our neighbors, and with the world. Christ commanded His disciples to become fishers of men. We must do likewise, and we must do so today. Tomorrow may indeed be too late.

Our commission is quite specific. We are told to be His witness to all nations. For us, as His disciples, to refuse any part of this commission frustrates the love of Jesus Christ, the Son of God.

Catherine Marshall

Jesus lives in the community; He only visits the church.

Anonymous

Notes

Notes

Notes

Notes

Notes

Notes

Notes